Pirkei Avot

Ethics of the Fathers

With Interpretation Of

Rabbeinu Yonah

Rabbi

Yonah Gerondi

simchatchaim.com

There is no known book without mistakes. Therefore, I ask in every language of application if anyone has any questions, comments, clarifications, corrections, please send to: **book@simchatchaim.com**

All material used in this section may not be used for commercial purposes, but only for study and teaching.

To get this book or books and information Email me at:

book@simchatchaim.com

Copyright©All Rights Reserved to

www.simchatchaim.com

YB"S©All rights reserved to the Editor

First Edition 2023

Pirkei Avot - Rabbeinu Yonah

Content of the book

PAGE

2.   Rabbeinu Yonah

5.   Chapter 1

45.   Chapter 2

93.   Chapter 3

137. Chapter 4

187. Chapter 5

227. Chapter 6

It is known that, neither the Rambam nor **Rabbeinu Yonah** did not write a commentary on Chapter 6 in Pirkei Avot.

Rabbeinu Yonah Gerondi

Yonah son of Avraham the Gironan, also known as Yonah of Girona and Rabbeinu Yonah was a Catalan rabbi and moralist, cousin of Nahmanides. He is most famous for his ethical work The Gates of Repentance and interpretation on Pirkei Avot- The Ethics of our Fathers.

Much of what is known about his life comes from a responsum by Solomon ben Simon Duran, one of his descendants.

Rabbeinu Yonah Gerondi Z"L came from Girona, in Catalonia [present-day Spain]. He was the most prominent pupil of Solomon ben Avraham of Montpellier, the leader of the opponents of Maimonides' philosophical works, and was one of the signers of the ban proclaimed in 1233 against The Guide for the Perplexed and the Sefer ha-Madda.

According to his pupil, Hillel ben Samuel, Gerondi was the instigator of the public burning of Maimonides writings by order of the authorities at Paris in 1233, and the indignation which this aroused among all classes of Jews was mainly directed against him. Subsequently, not forty days afterward, as a tradition has it, but in 1242 when twenty-four wagon-loads of Talmuds were burned at the same place where the philosophical writings of Maimonides had been destroyed, Rabbeinu Yonah saw the folly and danger of appealing to Christian ecclesiastical authorities on questions of Jewish doctrine, and publicly admitted in the synagogue of Montpellier that he had been wrong in all his acts against the works and fame of Maimonides.

As an act of repentance, he vowed to travel to Israel and prostrate himself on Maimonides' grave and implore his pardon in the presence of ten men for seven consecutive days. He left France with that intention, but was detained, first in Barcelona and later in Toledo. He remained in Toledo, and became one of the great Talmudical teachers of his time. In all his lectures he made a point of quoting from Maimonides, always mentioning his name with great reverence. Rabbeinu Yonah's sudden death from a rare disease was considered by many as a penalty for not having carried out the plan of his journey to the grave of Maimonides. However, some believe this was only a myth created by the followers of Maimonides. He died in Toledo in the Kingdom of Castile in November 1263. The text of his tombstone was later transcribed by Samuel David Luzzatto, with the month and possibly the day of his death being readable.

Rabbeinu Yonah left many works, of which only a few have been preserved. The Hiddushim to Alfasi on Berakhot which are ascribed to "Rabbenu Yonah" were in reality written in Gerondi's name by one, if not several, of his pupils. The Hiddushim originally covered the entire work of Alfasi, but only the portion mentioned has been preserved. Rabbeinu Yonah wrote novellæ on the Talmud, which are often mentioned in the responsa and decisions of his pupil Rabbi Solomon Aderet and of other great rabbis, and some of which are incorporated in the

Shiṭṭah Mekubbeẓet of Rabbi Bezalel Ashkenazi. Azulai had in his possession Rabbeinu Yonah novellae on the tractates Baba Batra and Sanhedrin, in manuscript. His novellæ on the first-named tractate have since been published under the name Aliyot de-Rabbenu Yonah while those on the last-named tractate form part of the collection of commentaries on the Talmud by ancient authors published by Avraham ben Eliezer ha-Levi under the title Sam Ḥayyim.

Rabbeinu Yonah's commentary on Pirkei Avot - Ethics of the Fathers is the greatest and most beautiful commentary. His is more in depth compared to those of Rashi and the Rambam.

The work Issur ve-Heter is wrongly attributed to Rabbeinu Yonah. A commentary by him on Proverbs, which is very highly praised, exists in manuscript. Among other minor unpublished works known to be his are Megillat Sefarim, Hilkot Ḥanukkah and Hilkot Yom Kippur.

But the fame of Rabbeinu Yonah chiefly rests on his moral and ascetic works, which, it is surmised, he wrote to atone for his earlier attacks on Maimonides and to emphasize his repentance.

Chapter 1

1. Moses received the Torah at Sinai, and transmitted it to Joshua, Joshua to the elders, and the elders to the prophets, and the prophets to the Men of the Great Assembly. They said three things: Be patient in the administration of justice, raise many disciples and make a fence round the Torah.

Rabbeinu Yonah

Moshe received the Torah from Sinai, etc.: I will begin the commentary on "Avot" of our great, pious and holy rabbi, Rabbi Yonah the son of Rabbi Avraham, may he be remembered for blessing. Our rabbis, may their memory be blessed, said - "One who wishes to be pious should fulfill the words of **Avotn** - the Ethics of the Fathers, and some said about it, the words of Damages". And since a person ascends the steps of piousness by doing one of these matters, they placed **Avot** in the Order of Damages. And even though they also said to fulfill the words of Blessings - Berakhot which is in the order of Seeds - Zeraim; because it speaks of the blessings on seeds and fruits, they placed it in that order. Furthermore, since it is the teachings of the Sanhedrin, they placed it in the order of the laws of Damages; and so [too], all the sages mentioned here until Rabban Yochanan ben Zakkai are all from the Sanhedrin.

Moshe received the Torah from Sinai and transmitted it to Yehoshua: Both the written Torah and the oral Torah. As the Torah was given with its explanation. As if it were not so, it would be impossible to understand its contents. As behold, it is written - "do not rob" and all of the laws of damages are within this negative commandment, and they themselves are the Torah that was received by Moshe at Sinai, even though

Pirkei Avot - Rabbeinu Yonah - Chapter 1

they were not written. And it is also written - "between a blood and a blood and between a judgement and a judgement and between an infection and an infection" - and many of the sightings of blood and many of the various judgments and so many of the infections are known to us by the transmission of this information. And they are not explained in writing because it is not allowed to be written. And it is written - "and I will give you the stone tablets and the Torah and the commandment" - **Torah** is the written Torah; "and the commandment" is the **oral Torah**. it comes out that you say that every commandment that He gave to Moshe at Sinai, was given with its explanation. And that which is written is what is called the written Torah and the explanation is what is called the oral Torah. And Moshe learned it from the mouth of the Mighty One.

And transmitted it to Yehoshua: As it is stated - "but his attendant, Joshua son of Nun, a youth, would not stir out of the tent."

And transmitted it to Yehoshua: As it is stated - "but his attendant, Joshua son of Nun, a youth, would not stir out of the tent."

And the Elders to the Prophets, and the Prophets transmitted it to the Men of the Great Assembly: And that is Ezra and his group. And some of the prophets of the Second Temple were in that group, as they said - "Rabbi Dosa ben Harkinas said, When Chaggai said these three things, he was sitting on this mortar." Hence the prophets of the Second Temple were there after the destruction, since Haggai the prophet was there. And the men of the Great Assembly transmitted it to the men of their generation. And the sages transmitted it to their children after them in each and every generation. And the transmission was from one sage to another, until all of the sages of Israel gathered and a suggestion was given from all of their mouths to write down the oral Torah. And so, they wrote and sealed the Talmud,

Pirkei Avot - Rabbeinu Yonah - Chapter 1

and afterwards nothing was added to it and nothing was taken away from it. And that generation also transmitted it to the Geonim and the transmission was from one Gaon to another, one rabbi to another - until this day.

They said three things: Be deliberate in judgment: They said this to teachers of legal decisions and decisors of legal decisions and decisors of litigation; that they should not rely on the first thought, but rather upon great deliberation and incisive investigation, so that they not err in their evaluation. As a man who is quick to make a decision is called a sinner - and even though he thought he was saying the truth, it is not [considered] accidental but rather is [considered] to be close to volitional, since he did not put it into his heart to say, the quick hearts do not understand to know. As error is found in all men, as the rabbis say - " Be careful in study, for an error in study is considered an intentional transgression." And about this matter, Shlomo, peace be upon him, stated - "If you see a man who thinks himself wise, there is more hope for a dullard than for him." And it is as the sages, may their memory be blessed, said - "One who is nonchalant about giving legal decisions is an imbecile, wicked, and arrogant in spirit." Therefore, it is incumbent upon a man who makes legal decisions to go back and forth on the matter and let his thought ripen and to hold on to it; as the matter that they said - that we should ripen a judgement, as through ripening and deliberation, he adds reasoning to his reasoning and sharpness to his sharpness, until he judges a completely true judgement. As he will see to say with the second thought that which he did not see with the first. And about this matter, Asaf stated - "As my heart ripened and my kidneys were silent," which is to say that after my heart has ripened and been sharp with wisdom and with my kidneys, I have been silent and have refined my understanding to know. As without this, I have not known, and this is my portion. And as it is after it, "I was a dolt, without knowledge; I was brutish toward You." And the reason they said, "Be deliberate in judgment," is in order to warn about litigation more than other legal decisions, as they are fundamental in the knowledge of Him, may He be blessed and elevated; and as Yirmiyahu the prophet stated - "ponder and know Me, for I am the Lord who makes kindness, justice, and equity in the world; for in these I delight, declares the Lord." And how can a man a ponder and know God, as it is not possible? However, with this have we known Him, by doing judgment and justice, since God does these. And that is what is stated - "He judged for the poor and needy - then all was well. That is truly knowing Me, declares the Lord." And it is written in another place - "And what does the Lord require of you? Only to do justice and to love kindness," since judgments are a pillar of the Torah. And from them the world is made firm, as is said in the Midrash - "It is written in front of The Ten Commandments, and they will judge the people at all times. And after the Ten Commandment, it is written. And these are the laws - There is a parable about this concerning a matron that was walking along the way and her armed guards were walking in front of her and behind her."

Raise up many disciples: As per the opinion of Beit Hillel. This is like the matter that we have learned, - "Beit Shammai say, 'We only teach a student who is fit, modest, proper and who fears Heaven, as it is stated - "All darkness waits for his treasured ones." And Beit Hillel say, 'We teach everyone: One hundred so that ten good ones will come out from them; and ten so that two will come out of them; and two, "since you do not know which will be proper, this one or that one or if they will both be equally good." And so, was there a story of Hillel, who brought together all of his students and said to them, 'Are all of you here?' They said [back] to him, 'Yes.' One of his students said to him, 'All of them are here except the smallest one.' He said to them, 'Let the small one come, for the future generation will be conducted by him.' And they brought Rabban Yochanan ben Zakkai. Behold that one should not push off the small ones for the bigger ones, since the kids will become goats." And about this matter the rabbis, may their memory be blessed, expounded - "Sow your seed in the morning, and don't hold back your hand in the evening - if you have raised disciples in your youth, raise disciples in your old age." Behold that the multiplication of disciples is a very good thing and a merit to the teacher.

And make a fence for the Torah: As the matter that is stated - "And you shall guard My guarding"; which is to say, make a guarding for my guarding. And a fence is a great thing and it is praiseworthy to make a fence for the commandments so that the one who fears the word of God not stumble in them. Hence one who observes the words of the sages, may their memory be blessed - which are the fences for the commandments of the Torah - has shown more love for this fear than one who does the commandment itself. As the doing of the commandments does not prove fear like the one who observes the fences, since he is careful from the start not to come to error. However, the one who does the commandment but does not observe the fence shows us that if it is good in his eyes to do the commandment, yet it is not bad in his eyes if he errs in it; and that he is not concerned about the fear that he will make a breach in it, and 'one who makes a breach will be bitten by a snake.' Behold that the words of the sages, may their memory be blessed, are pillars and 'trees' in the fear of Heaven; which is a foundation of the world and a fundamental principle of virtue. And all of the commandments are appetizers for it, as they said in the Midrash - "For your love is more delightful than wine - the words of the scribes are more beloved than the wine of Torah."

2. Shimon the Righteous was one of the last of the men of the great assembly. He used to say: the world stands upon three things: the Torah, the Temple service, and the practice of acts of piety.

Rabbeinu Yonah

Shimon the Righteous was from the remnants of the Great Assembly. And he was a high priest, as they said in Tractate - that he had gone out dressed with the priestly garments in front of Alexander the Great, and Alexander went down and bowed before him. His servants said to him, "Our master, A king like you should bow down to this Jew?" He said back to them, "I see the image of this one in war and I am victorious."

He would say, "On three things the world stands": This means to say that because of these things the world was created. As below - it states, "On three the things the world subsists," and they are not those that it mentions here. Hence, we need to explain that when they said "stands," it means that the world was created for them, since they are the will of the Holy One, blessed be He. This means to say that the world was created for His creatures that in the future would fulfill His will in front of Him through these things. And these three are a great pillar, such that on account of them, we are able to get to all of the other things that the sages, may their memory be blessed, said that the world stands because of them.

On the Torah: As it stated about it, as it is stated - "He who seeks what is good pursues what is pleasing." And good is only Torah, and because of it the world was created, as it is stated - "Were it not for My covenant, night and day, etc. And this is what Shlomo, peace be upon him, said - "The Lord created me at the beginning of His course, as the first of His works of old" - I was created before the whole world and because of me, all of the creations were created - in order to observe me.

On the service: As the Holy One, blessed be He, chose Israel from all of the nations and the Land of Israel from all of the lands, and He chose Jerusalem from all of the Land of Israel and He chose Zion from Jerusalem, as it is stated - "As the Lord chose Zion, He desired it for His habitation." And He chose the House of Choice from everything for the sake of the service, about which it is written, "desire" - as it states - "desirous in front of God." Behold that because of the service the whole world was created. Then, due to our sins, the Temple was destroyed and the service was annulled. And prayer is now for us in its place, as the sages, may their memory be blessed, said - "And to serve him with all your hearts - what service is there in the heart, one should say this is prayer." And this is what it states - "Lord, open my lips," as King David said this verse about the sin of Batsheva which was volitional, and one cannot bring a sacrifice for volitional sins. And about this he stated - "Since You do not want me to bring sacrifices; You do not desire burnt offerings." Had I been able to bring a sacrifice to atone for myself, I would have brought it. Now that I cannot, Lord, open my lips and let my mouth say your praise, and accept my prayer in place of a sacrifice and let it atone me for my sin. Also, for us that do not have a sacrifice to atone for us - not accidental sins and not volitional sins - Lord, open my lips and accept our prayers in place of the sacrifices.

And on acts of lovingkindness: As the matter that they said - "Acts of lovingkindness are greater than charity tsedekah; since lovingkindness is both with the poor and with the wealthy but charity is only with the poor. Great is lovingkindness since it is both with one's body and with one's money, but charity is only with one's money." And this is what they said - "One who gives a small coin to a poor man is blessed in six ways and one who comforts him with words is blessed in eleven." And pertinent to acts of lovingkindness is to inspect the poor and to make a distinction between the good and the bad and to give preference to the modest and those that fear God over others who are not like them, even if we must give charity to all. And it is like Yirmiyahu, peace be upon him, stated - "let them be made to stumble before You; act against them in Your hour of wrath!" - even in the time that they do charity, make them stumble that they should give it in the incorrect place. And acts of lovingkindness are even to the wealthy, to lend them money at a time when it is not found in their hand and to give them advice, as King Shlomo said, - "Oil and incense gladden the heart, but the sweetness of a friend is better than one's own counsel." This is to say, just like oil and incense gladden the heart, so too does one's friend become delighted by personal advice; and when he gives him good advice, he is gladdened by it. And this trait of kindness brings God's satisfaction in front of Him, and for it was the world created - in order to do it. And about it Shlomo said in his wisdom - "Righteousness exalts a nation; Sin is a reproach to any people" - and adjacent to it, "The king favors a capable servant" - the will of the Holy One, blessed be He is only for Israel, who investigate how to do the things that are desirable in front of Him.

Pirkei Avot - Rabbeinu Yonah - Chapter 1

3. Antigonus a man of Socho received the oral tradition from Shimon the Righteous. He used to say: do not be like servants who serve the master in the expectation of receiving a reward, but be like servants who serve the master without the expectation of receiving a reward, and let the fear of Heaven be upon you.

Rabbeinu Yonah רבינו יונה

Antigonos, man of Sokho, etc., "Do not be as servants who are serving the master in order to receive a reward": As this is not complete service, as he is not doing it for his master, but rather in order to receive a reward.

Rather be as servants who are serving the master in order not to receive a reward: Editor's note: In my opinion, here there should be the words, "And it is difficult according to this textual variant." Since a person should not do the commandment with the understanding that he will not receive a reward for them. But rather the correct textual variant is "not in order to receive a reward" - that he should not do the commandments for the sake of the reward, even though he should think that there will be recompense for his service. However, it appears to me that the variant of the books is the main one that we should follow: As we find such service among people, such that a purchased slave is obligated to do service without receiving reward. So too, a man must serve God in order not to receive a reward, but rather because of the kindness that He has already performed for him. And also due to the greatness of the Master, that He is fitting for this, and this is the service of God - may He be blessed and elevated - from love, as it is stated - "And you shall love the Lord." And what is complete service among people? One who wants to serve his friend because of his love for him from earlier days, and even if he knows that he will not give him a reward. And with this type of love should a person love the service of God. And therefore, the Mishnah placed it adjacent to the matter of fear and stated,

And may the fear of Heaven be upon you: To serve God from fear and from love, like a servant that serves his master because of his greatness and also keeps in mind that he can punish him. And it comes out that he serves him from fear - not because of his fear from the punishment, but rather because of the greatness of the master, whereby he has the ability to punish.

4. Yose ben Yoezer a man of Zeredah and Yose ben Yohanan a man of Jerusalem received the oral tradition from them [i.e. Shimon the Righteous and Antigonus]. Yose ben Yoezer used to say: let thy house be a house of meeting for the Sages and sit in the very dust of their feet, and drink in their words with thirst.

Rabbeinu Yonah

Yose ben Yoezer, man of Tsreida, and Yose ben Yochanan, man of Jerusalem, received from him: From Shimon the Righteous and Antigonos, man of Sokho.

Yose ben Yoezer says, may your house be a meeting house for Sages: It means to say, a house that the sages will gather there when they need to speak, one with the other. And this can only be in the house of a great and important man. As were it in the house of a lesser man, when they would say to the sage to go there, perhaps he would not want, since [for] him, 'a base one is disgraceful in his eyes; and he does not honor those that fear the Lord.

become dirty in the dust of their feet: That he treats them with honor, as it was their way to stand in front of the sage. And some of them would sit on benches in the house of study and some of them would sit in front of them on the floor at the dust of their feet, as they said - "All the days that that student apprenticed in sitting, I apprenticed in standing." And this is what he stated: Be honored among all of the creatures, but honor the sages.

And drink their words thirstily: And this is like it is stated - "A sated person disdains honey, but to a hungry man anything bitter seems sweet." The soul of one who is sated from words of Torah and does not desire them will disdain them - even if they tell him pearls of Torah. But one who is hungry for them, and desires to hear them, will find them sweet in his mouth and will be happy about it - even if he is told something without an explanation - since he knows that it is true, as his teacher said it.

5. Yose ben Yochanan a man of Jerusalem used to say: Let thy house be wide open, and let the poor be members of thy household. Engage not in too much conversation with women. They said this with regard to one's own wife, how much more does the rule apply, with regard to another man's wife. From here the Sages said: as long as a man engages in too much conversation with women, he causes evil to himself, he neglects the study of the Torah, and in the end, he will inherit gehinnom.

Rabbeinu Yonah

Yose ben Yochanan, man of Jerusalem, says, may your home be open wide: Some say that this means that there be largess found in his house for needy people. Or the explanation is that his house be like the house of our father Avraham, peace be upon him - such that his house be on the road in a tight spot so that passers by should come in to there; and that it should be open on four sides, so that from all sides that they come, they will find an open door and they will turn into it, as Job stated -"I opened my doors to the road."

May the poor be members of your household: This is expounded in two ways. Instead of buying slaves and supporting them, he should use poor people and support them and he will not need to expend money. So that it comes out that he will profit and do a commandment, good deed. Another explanation: And also, that the poor will be accustomed to his house and stay there without embarrassment, as a result of his showing them a happy face and giving them permission to everything that is his, like a man would give to his children and to the people of his home.

And do not increase conversation with the woman: As conversation with women brings one to thoughts of sin and neglect of Torah study.

They so stated with his wife; all the more so with the wife of his friend. Our master and teacher Rashi wrote, as it is written in the Fathers According to Rabbi Nathan, they said this about his menstruant wife, all the more so regarding the wife of his fellow. It means to say, that he not increase words with his menstruant wife, lest his impulse overcomes him and he comes to a mishap; and all the more so with the wife of his fellow, about whom his impulse pressures him even more. As if they said it with the one that will be permissible for him tomorrow - and it appears to him like 'bread in his basket' - all the more so with another woman, whom the impulse desires, as the matter that it stated - stolen waters are sweet. But it appears to be explained according to its simple meaning, they so stated with his wife, not to ever accustom her to many words, so that she not be found with him every day. As a man should not be with his wife for his pleasure, but [rather] to fulfill the commandment; so as to distinguish between man and beast, as they said in - concerning a man with a nocturnal emission, "So that they not be with their wives like chickens." And that is the trait of separation which brings one to the highest levels, as we say, "Separation brings to purity."

And neglects the words of Torah: As the thought of Torah is not firm in his eyes so long as his heart is focused on the woman and upon her conversation, as they are two thoughts that the heart does not tolerate together.

And, in his end, he inherits Geihinam [hell]: As in the end, he comes to sin: Since he follows the whims of his heart and increases words, certainly it should be with the he will sin and descend to the pit. And this is what Shlomo - peace be upon him stated - "I find woman more bitter than death; she is all traps; her heart is snares and her hands are fetters." This means to say that death removes him from the world - from the small life of the world - but woman destroys his soul for ever and ever. Behold, 'she is more bitter than death.' "She is all traps and snares": When a man observes a woman, he is

Pirkei Avot - Rabbeinu Yonah - Chapter 1

caught in her net, which is her trap, and he cannot escape from her. As the man sees that which his heart desires and he does not see what will happen to him from her in the end of days. As the lyricist Rabbi Yehudah HaLevi said, "The seduced dove travels in the wilderness; it sees the grain but it does not see the trap." "Her heart is snares" - when she desires a man in her heart, even if he does not desire her and it is [just] the bad fortune of this man that caused her to desire him. "Her hands are fetters" - because if she grabs him with her hands, he is already taken into the 'prison' and he no longer has a way to fix it. "He who is pleasing to God escapes her, and he who is displeasing is caught by her" as the Holy One, blessed be He, protects the righteous and does not present them something through which they might stumble; but the sinner, who does not distance himself from evil paths and whose heart is not complete, chances upon a matter like this.

Pirkei Avot - Rabbeinu Yonah - Chapter 1

6. Joshua ben Perahiah and Nittai the Arbelite received the oral tradition from them. Joshua ben Perahiah used to say: appoint for thyself a teacher, and acquire for thyself a companion and judge all men with the scale weighted in his favor.

Rabbeinu Yonah רבינו יונה

Yehoshua ben Perachiah and Nitai of Arbel received from them: From Yose ben Yoezer and Yosef ben Yochanan.

Yehoshua ben Perachia says. Make for yourself a mentor, acquire for yourself a friend: As even if you know as much as him, make him a mentor upon you, since a person remembers better what he learned from his mentor than what a person learned on his own. And also, because sometimes he will understand a thing better and it will come out that he will teach him - even as they are both equal in wisdom.

Acquire for yourself a friend: A person needs three things from a good friend. One is for words of Torah, as it stated - "I have learned much from my teachers and more from my friends than from my teachers." And the second is for commandments. As even if his friend is not more pious than he and there are times that he does what is not in order. Yet it is only when he derives pleasure from something that he does the sin, but it is not his desire and his will that his friend do it - as he derives no enjoyment from this. And it is like they said - "And a man will not sin if it is not for himself." It comes out that both of them will repent, each one according to the word of his friend. And the third is regarding advice that he can take, that he be one who arouses a counselor for help in all of his affairs and to take good counsel from him and to be his confidant. Since he is his ally, he will not reveal his secrets to others so as not to confound his plan and not even to those that appear to him to be friends; for is the appearance of love evident on their faces? And about this Shlomo, peace be upon him, stated - "Plans are foiled for want of counsel, but they succeed through many advisers." And that which he said, "acquire for yourself a friend" with an expression of acquisition is to say that if he does not find him for free, he should acquire him with his money and expend his assets in order to get to a good friend; or that he should acquire him with words of appeasement and with a soft way of talking. And so, he should not be exacting about his words and he should tolerate the words of his mouth; even when he says something against him, he should not return a response. As without this, he will not keep the friendship, since the opinions of people are different. And sometimes he will seek something, but his friend who is like himself will say, "See, I do not [consider] this to be fit." And if he doesn't listen to his friend, he will certainly pass him up, the friendship will unravel. And this is what Shlomo, peace be upon him, stated - "He who seeks love covers errors, but he who harps on a matter alienates a leader." He meant to say, one who covers when his friend errs, seeks love - as through this, their love is preserved, as he tolerates his errors. But if he harps about the matter with his friend, he speaks against him and repeats it and says, "See what this one said; what he said about me, he 'alienates the leader' - he certainly alienates his leader from him, meaning to say, his friend.

And judge every person as meritorious: This is speaking about a person about whom we do not know if he is righteous or if he is evil; or if we know that he is a moderate person, sometimes doing evil and sometimes doing good. And if he does something that can make us judge him unfavorably and also judge him favorably in our understanding - or even if, towards according to what appears, it leans more towards the side of guilt - if he can judge him favorably from one aspect of the matter, he should say - "His intentions were good." But these words are not applicable to the completely righteous or the completely evil. As with the righteous person, even with an action that is completely evil and leans toward guilt in every aspect, we should judge him favorably and say, "'It was a mistake that came out from the hand of the ruler,' and behold he regretted and observed it and already requested forgiveness." And it is like the sages, may their memory be blessed, said - "If you see a Torah scholar who sinned at night, do not ruminate about him during the day, lest he has repented. Lest comes into your mind? But rather, I will say he certainly repented." The explanation of "'Lest' comes into your mind?" is that since he is a Torah scholar and up until now, no corrupt thing has come to his hand; he certainly repented right away. You behold from here that one should never judge the perfectly righteous person unfavorably. And about him there is no reason to say, "judge every person as meritorious." And he also did not speak about the completely evil person. Even if his actions are completely good and it is not evident to be concerned about him regarding an angle of iniquity, a person should judge him unfavorably and say, "He did it on the surface 'and his inside is not like his outside.'" And it is like it is stated - "Though he be fair-spoken do not trust him, for seven abominations are in his heart." And so too wrote Rambam, may his memory be blessed. And about this King Shlomo stated in his wisdom - "The righteous one observes the house of the wicked man; he subverts the wicked to the bad." He meant to say, people think that because the righteous do not know how to do evil, [hence] they do not recognize they ways of the evil - as they do not understand those that do it. And the matter is not like this, as 'the righteous one observes the house of the wicked,' and knows and recognizes and monitors the evil of his ways more than other people who know about it, but don't pay attention to it. "He subverts the wicked to the bad" - when the righteous person sees the action of the evildoers which appear to be in a good path, he subverts it and pushes it towards his judgment to say that he has done wrong - since he did not intend [to do] a commandment, but rather to place himself among those assumed to be good.

7. Nittai the Arbelite used to say: keep a distance from an evil neighbor, do not become attached to the wicked, and do not abandon faith in divine retribution.

Rabbeinu Yonah

נתאי הארבלי אומר הרחק משכן רע. לשוכר בתים ולקונה עבדים אמרו. כי כאשר ישאל איש תחלה על דירה ובמקום דוחק כך יש לו לשאול על השכנים אם רעים הם ירחק מהם ולטובים יקרב:

Nitai of Arbel says: Distance yourself from a bad neighbor: He said it to renters of houses and purchasers of slaves. As when a person first asks about the house and the tightness of the place, he should ask about the neighbors - if they are evil, he should distance himself from them, and he should come close to the good ones.

Do not befriend an evildoer: As it brings a great punishment, which has nothing like it. Since if he transgresses a great sin, he did one sin; but this one has a portion in all of the sins that the evildoer does. And it comes out that he does many great and huge sins. And even if his hands are tied and he does not benefit from them, woe to the evildoer and woe to his neighbor - as 'he sins and his neighbor is flogged.' As so is it explained in The Fathers According to Rabbi Nathan - "Anyone who clings to evildoers - even though he does not do like their deeds - takes recompense like them; and one who clings to the righteous - even though he does not do like their deeds - takes recompense like them." And about this it is stated - "As you have made a partnership, etc., the Lord will break up your work."

And do not despair: He made these two things adjacent and said, do not befriend an evildoer, because you need not despair from punishment. And do not say in your heart, "He is still standing in tranquility and times are good for him - I will befriend him and when his good fortune changes, I will distance myself from him." And you cannot do this, as you will not know what each new day will bring, and his time will come in an instant, and you will be taken with him; when he begins to fall, he and all of his friends will fall. And also, do not say, "I will show him love outwardly, but I will not love him in my heart." As it is also evil for you to flatter him, since it is a sin to flatter evildoers in this world. And about this matter Shlomo stated - "Fear the Lord, my son, and the king, and do not mix with changers. For their time comes suddenly; the doom of both, who can foreknow?" The explanation is that he made adjacent the fear of the Lord, my son, and the king to the fear of a flesh and blood king as a metaphor relating the fear of the body from that which is perceived by the eye with the fear of the soul from that which is invisible. And he said when you see that the king hates all those who love his enemies and that he metes out bad to him, asks who is it that filled his heart to love the enemy of the king, and does to him the same thing that he does to his enemy; know that so too the Holy One, blessed be He, does to all those who mix with the changers - that is to say, those that change the Torah and the commandments. As the word **change** here is transitive, as in - "After my word, things were not changed." And when the changers are struck, their friends will also be collected with them - Should one give aid to the wicked and befriend those who hate the Lord? For this, it shall be upon you. "As his time comes suddenly" and you will not be able to escape for your life. "And the doom of both, who can foreknow," meaning to say, the doom of the king's hater and the doom of the hater of the Holy One, blessed be He. Who knows when it will come to them, and so no man can be careful to befriend them and to save his own life.

8. Judah ben Tabbai and Shimon ben Shetach received the oral tradition from them. Judah ben Tabbai said: do not as a judge, play the part of an advocate; and when the litigants are standing before you, look upon them as if they were both guilty; and when they leave your presence, look upon them as if they were both innocent, when they have accepted the judgement.

<u>Rabbeinu Yonah רבינו יונה</u>

Yehuda ben Tabai and Shimon ben Shetach received from them: From Yehoshua ben Perachiah and Nitai of Arbel.

Yehuda ben Tabai says, "Do not make yourself like the judges' advisers": He means to say a head, as it is stated in - "And Efron was sitting among the children of Chet - on that very day, they appointed him arkhi," meaning to say the head of the judges. And also, in the section of "Yaakov sent messengers" - **arkhi** is the head of the thieves. And also, in Arukh, you will find that arkhi is explained like this there. And the explanation of this is, do not make yourself like the judge's advisers, that people should ask you and you tell them the laws; and after they hear it from you, they go to other judges for judgment and they say to them, "The head of the judges has already told us that this is the law." Do not make yourself like them. And from Rambam there is another explanation: "Do not make yourself like the judges' advisers" - He did not speak here about someone who teaches false claims to his friend and how to present them, since such a person is completely evil. And it is not necessary to say that a person not do this on account that they will suspect him and speak badly about him, as this is a great sin and nothing more need be said about it. Rather, it is one that organizes the claims of someone and arranges the laws and reveals the verdict of a case to an individual - as it is not fitting to do this since they will suspect him and speak badly about him. This is like that story of Rabbi Yochanan - wherein at the beginning he reasoned, "do not ignore your flesh", and at the end he reasoned, it is different with an important man.

And when the litigants are before you, they should be like evildoers in your eyes: That your heart should not lean towards one of them, and that you not think that he is righteous in his case. As if so, you will never judge a case truthfully, since your heart is unfettered towards this one, and you will not be able to see his guilt. Rather they should be in your eyes as if they were both evil and making false claims. And let not your heart lean to one of them, so that the matter come under the correct light.

And when they are excused from before you, they should be meritorious in your eyes - when they have accepted the judgment: This is a measure of piety, since you know that one of them made a false claim. Still, he should not be in your eyes ever assumed to be a liar and a difficult litigant. And it is not fitting to suspect him, since he accepted the verdict upon himself and left the court guilty. And one should think that he repented and he doesn't have in mind to do this again all the days of his life.

9. Shimon ben Shetach used to say: be thorough in the interrogation of witnesses, and be careful with your words, lest from them they learn to lie.

Rabbeinu Yonah

Shimon ben Shatach says, "Examine the witnesses thoroughly: To examine and cross-examine them many times. And through this you will reveal the secret, since 'with many words sin will not be averted' and he will learn from their words if they are testifying falsely.

But be careful with your words, lest from them they learn to lie: As when you examine them about a matter, you can speak your words in such a way that they will understand in what way they will be found guilty in their trial and learn from your words what lies they need to make to win the case.

10. Shemaiah and Abtalion received the oral tradition from them. Shemaiah used to say: love work, hate acting the superior, and do not attempt to draw near to the ruling authority.

Rabbeinu Yonah

Shemayah and Avtalyon received from them. Shemayah says, "Love work": So that a man not be idle from work, since idleness brings a person to ennui - and that is a trait of illness, as it is stated about it - "The craving of a lazy man kills him, for his hands refuse to do." It means to say, when he accustoms his limbs to be idle from work, his hands refuse, since habit rules over them. And it also states about it - "From the winter the lazy man does not plow; at harvest time he seeks, and there is nothing." As he thinks when he is idle from work that it is rest for him, but it is the opposite; as it is with exertion that he will have rest. As with the winter he will rest and stay in his house and not plow and seek to reap and gather the grain when there is none and die of hunger. But the one who plows in the winter - he who tills his land will be sated with bread, as a man cannot reach rest without exertion first. But he who pursues vanities' and pursues the ones that sit in the corners idle from work 'will be sated with poverty.

Hate lordship: He made this adjacent to the activity of work, as they are one topic - that he hates lordship and the advantage of the idle ones, as their end is to come to the trait of poverty. But rather he should be involved in his work the whole day, as it said - "Flay a carcass in the marketplace and eat from your wage, and do not say, I am a priest, I am an important man." And about this King Shlomo, peace be upon him, stated - "Better to be a lowly one and a servant to himself than to be honored and have no food." And the explanation of **lowly one** is not like its literal understanding, but rather it is the opposite of honored lordship.

And do not become familiar with the government: As service for the government is very difficult. And regardless, once he accepts the yoke of the king, his end is to break the yoke of the kingdom of Heaven and to refrain from this commandment. Since he will be afraid of the government and his work will be extensive, he will make the service of God a farce in the face of this work. And also, at the end, they will strip him of his assets without gain, as they only bring someone close for their own purpose. And regardless, once he accepts the yoke of a king of flesh and blood at one time, he can not longer do that which the Master requires.

11. Abtalion used to say: Sages be careful with your words, lest you incur the penalty of exile, and be carried off to a place of evil waters, and the disciples who follow you drink and die, and thus the name of heaven becomes profaned.

Rabbeinu Yonah

Avtalyon says, "Sages, be careful with your words, lest you become obligated in an obligation of exile. Rambam, may his memory be blessed, wrote in a correct way in his commentary on Avot: "Be careful with your words," to explain your words so that you not leave room for heresy, "lest you become obligated in an obligation of exile and are exiled to the place of evil waters" - the place of heretics that reveal the faces of Torah that are not appropriate, and extract from your words, things that are not so.

And the students who follow after you will drink. As they will hear your words and not understand and rely upon the words of the heretics who explain your words according to their opinions, and they will reason that this was your opinion, "and thus the name of Heaven is profaned."

12. Hillel and Shammai received the oral tradition from them. Hillel used to say: be of the disciples of Aaron, loving peace and pursuing peace, loving mankind and drawing them close to the Torah.

Rabbeinu Yonah

Hillel and Shammai received from them: From Shemayah and Avtalyon.

Hillel says, "Be of the disciples of Aharon, loving peace and pursuing peace, loving the creatures and bringing them closer to Torah." He means to say that he loves truth and peace in his heart and pursues it with the actions of his hands. As there are people that love it in their hearts that don't trouble themselves to bring peace to the world and don't walk in the paths of peace. But those that do actions and bring peace between a man and his friend and love to do this work, as it is stated - "seek peace and pursue it", those are from the students of Aharon, who would act like this.

Loving the creatures and bringing them closer to Torah: When Aharon would sense that a person had sinned in private, he would go to him and befriend him and make him into his friend. And the sinner would put in his heart that if Aharon would know the hidden matters in my heart, would he ever want my friendship? Rather, it is that I am assumed by him to be a proper man and one who does the commandments. However, if he knew my bad thought, he would distance himself from me - from befriending an evildoer like me today. And [so] he would regret his evil and contemplate repentance. And this is very effective and beneficial for him in undoing his evil thought, as is stated - "He walked with Me in peace and righteousness, and brought many back from iniquity."

13. He also used to say: one who makes his name great causes his name to be destroyed; one who does not add to his knowledge causes it to cease; one who does not study the Torah deserves death; one who makes unworthy use of the crown of learning shall pass away.

Rabbeinu Yonah

He would say, "Spread a name, lose his name:" He means to say, a man that is proud and his name goes out in the world due to his pride and his greatness and he makes for himself a name like the names of the world's greats in opposition to the great Name that is permanent in pride; this way, will he lose his name in a great loss and he will not be remembered and he will not be counted.

And one who does not increase knowledge ceases yasef. One who is wise but does not want to add wisdom to his wisdom, and says in his heart, "I have already learned all of the Torah entirely and I have seen its ways and its paths. What is there for me in this pain to trouble myself in my fleeting days and what more is there for me to understand that I have not understood?" May it be His will that this man should die and be gathered to his people. And why should he live any more, since he has already gotten up from studying?

And one who does not study is liable to die: One who has not studied at all is compared to a beast. As why was he created in the world? To understand and give ruling of the Torah, whose ways are ways of pleasantness. And it is not fitting that the one that never learned Torah and continues to maintain his evil this way live even one day and even one hour.

And one who makes use of the crown of learning passes away: Behold the one who gets honor from the crown of

Pirkei Avot - Rabbeinu Yonah - Chapter 1

Torah and benefits from its honor and makes it like a means to accomplish his needs, perishes, as it is learned later - "Do not make it the Torah into a crown with which to aggrandize yourself, and not into a spade with which to dig into them. And thus, Hillel used to say: And one who makes use of the crown of learning passes away.

14. He also used to say: If I am not for myself, who is for me? But if I am for my own self only, what am I? And if not now, when?

Rabbeinu Yonah

Hillel used to say: If I am not for me, who will be for me? If I don't rebuke myself to be assiduous about the commandments, who is there to rebuke me and make me assiduous? Since the prompting of others is only good on a temporary basis. But when the person motivates himself each and every day, he increases to think of thoughts in order to do the work of God. And there is no forgetting before him, when his heart desires it, and it is a straight path in front of a person.

And when I am for myself alone, what am I? I still cannot reach one thousandth of what I am obligated to do. And they made a parable about this: To what is the thing similar? To a king that gave his field to his servants and agreed with them that his portion would be thirty **kor** [A size of about 250 liters]. They toiled and they brought him five kor. The king said to them, "But didn't I agree with you that it be thirty kor?" They said to him, "Our master, the king, the field that you gave us was of low quality. We toiled greatly on it and we were not able to get out from it more than five kor." So, did they say in front of the Holy One, blessed be He, "It is the evil impulse that you have given us from our youth, as it is stated - the impulse of man's heart is evil from his youth. And even when a man toils greatly to do what is straight in the eyes of God, a man only accomplishes a small part of what he is obligated to do." And this is what is stated - "For He knows our impulse; He is mindful that we are dust." Since were it not that He made the evil impulse powerful in man - even without his working hard and pursuing the commandments - he would do many of them. [It would be] like in a high-quality field - even if they did not toil in the work of his land - something would come out of it. But now that he knows that even if he toils greatly, he will only attain a small amount because of the evil impulse that corrupts his body; [then] all the more so if he does not toil, his soul will remain empty of the commandments, like a poor-quality field if one does not toil in it. And if he does not fertilize it and plow it, nothing will come out of it. And about this is it stated - "I passed by the field of a lazy man, by the vineyard of a man lacking sense. It was all overgrown with thorns; its surface was covered with chickweed, and its stone fence lay in ruins." And for this reason, he made the motivation of others adjacent to the motivation of himself and said, " If I am not for me, who will be for me," but if I don't toil and motivate myself to pursue the commandments, I will stay devoid of them - since, even "when I am for myself" and toil in them, I only reach a small portion of the many portions and what do I reach. mah ani can mean both "what am I" and what do I if I don't toil at all?

And if not now, then when? Such that he not says, I will occupy myself with my work today and tomorrow I will turn to and occupy myself with self-improvement. Since maybe he will not turn to [it]. And even if he does turn to it, that day went, left and he removed it from the work of God. And he will not be able to make it up all the days of his life, since he is obligated to improve himself and to be occupied by the commandment all of the days that he is living upon the earth, and he does not have the right to avoid this work - not even for a moment. And there is also included in this expression, "If not now," in the days of my youth, "then when?" If I leave it until my old age and hoariness, I will not be able to do it. And about this matter, David, peace be upon him, stated - "For our sons are like saplings, well-tended in their youth." He meant to say that when the sapling is small, a person can grow it to be a straight tree and not be crooked. However, after it grows crooked, it is very difficult to fix. And so too when a person is still young, it is easy for him to be on a good path and to turn from evil, but when he grows old with his evil, it is difficult in his eyes to leave it, as it is written -

"Teach a lad according to his way; also, when he will grow old, he not sway from it." And it is also, written - "since a man is a tree of the field." And also, because repentance in old age is not full repentance. Since at that time, the impulse is not strong and desire is benign and the soul does not enjoy - and he does not desire - sinful pleasures. And this is the reason for his repentance. And about this matter is it stated - "And remember your Creator in the days of your youth, before those days of bad come and those years arrive of which you will say, 'I have no desire in them.'"

15. Shammai used to say: make your study of the Torah a fixed practice; speak little, but do much; and receive all men with a pleasant countenance.

Rabbeinu Yonah

Shammai says, "Make your Torah fixed": As they said in The Fathers According to Rabbi Nathan - "Anyone who makes his Torah study primary and his work secondary is made primary in the world to come. And anyone that makes his Torah study secondary and his work primary will be made secondary in the world to come. This means to say, even though he did not do a sin, but he did not make Torah primary - even if he was fit to be in the Garden of Eden, he will be secondary there.

Say little and do much: When you promise your friend to do something for him, tell him a little and do much for him, and that is in the way of ethics and piety. And we have learned [it] from our father Avraham, peace be upon him, as it is written - "And let me fetch a morsel of bread"; and afterwards - "And he took curds and milk and the calf, etc." Another explanation: "say little and do much" - and that is a lofty virtue. And our rabbis, may their memory be blessed, learned it from the blessed Holy One, blessed be He, who only promised with two letters, as it is stated - "I will judge [dan, a word which is written with only two letters]; and delivered them with twenty-seven words, as it is stated - "Or has any god ventured to go and take for himself one nation from the midst of another, etc." And about this Rabbi Saadia Gaon, my-his memory be blessed, said, "If in promising our fathers with two letters, he did for them many miracles and wonders; with the salvation in the future to come about which have been written many pages and many manuscripts and many books of promises and many consolations in Jeremiah in the Prophets, how much the more so will it be that His actions will be more wondrous than that which He promised - our soul knows this well. And a person should know and consider the matter and to put into his heart that there will be a great reward for him because of the promises".

And receive every person with a pleasant countenance: That he shows them a happy face, so that the spirit of creations find pleasure from him. Another explanation: "and receive" - that he should distance himself from the trait of anger which is a very bad trait and conduct himself with the trait of good will, in such a way that people will be satisfied with him. This is proper and well-accepted. About this our sages, may their memory be blessed, said in the way of ethical teachings, "Do you want to be liked? Like that which you don't like." As a person cannot accomplish that the people of the world will like him if he does not forego his traits. And if he does not forego his wants for the sake of their wants, he must negate his will for the sake of the will of others. And with this, he will have many friends and guard himself from the injuries of people. As they will hate and seek to hurt one who shows them an angry face.

16. Rabban Gamaliel used to say: appoint for thyself a teacher, avoid doubt, and do not make a habit of tithing by guesswork.

Rabbeinu Yonah

Rabban Gamliel says, "Make for yourself a mentor, remove yourself from doubt": He means to say that he should take his colleague as his mentor - even though he is not wiser than he, and even if he has not even reached' the first one's wisdom - in order that he remove himself from doubt. And in Talmud Yerushalmi Moed Katan it states, "Go and bring me an elder from the marketplace and I will rely upon him and permit it to you." As there are times when a sage will be in doubt about a ruling and he will not know what to say: If he permits, maybe it is forbidden and a mishap will occur through him; and if he forbids what is permitted, it will come out that he will cause a loss of money to Israel, whereas the Torah is concerned about it. Therefore, he should make his colleague a mentor and ask him about his questions. And he will make the ruling upon his mouth, even if the matter is simple to him and even if it is a permissive ruling, even when he is not as great as he in wisdom. And thus, did the Geonim say, "In anything where it is a doubt to one and clear to the other, the law is like the one to whom it is clear, even if it is a student before his mentor."

And do not frequently tithe by estimation: That he not tithes his fruits by estimation. If he wants to tithe what he has measured out generously to be more than the tenth, it comes out that, that which is beyond the tenth is still revel a forbidden mixture that requires separation to render it permissible that is not tithed until he puts his eyes to it to tithe it, and it comes out that there is a corruption of this tithe. And this matter is a metaphor for the matter of reasoning, in which a person should not do it by estimation, but rather in the way of principles and to come to full knowledge. And this is not the case with all reasonings. As there is one that is nuanced and the sage - even though his reasoning leans to the side that he understands - recognizes that another sage can [see] it in a different way. It is just that his way looks more correct in his eyes. And there is another reasoning that a sage innovates and recognizes and knows that it is logically correct and necessary, has no other angles and that no other sage would disagree. And the one who understands will understand this. And for this reason, was this matter made adjacent to the teaching, "Make for yourself a mentor, remove yourself from doubt" - as the two teachings are based on almost the same rationale.

17. Shimon, his son, used to say: all my days I grew up among the sages, and I have found nothing better for a person than silence. Study is not the most important thing, but actions; whoever indulges in too many words brings about sin.

Rabbeinu Yonah

Shimon, his son, says, "All my days I grew up among the Sages": And I have observed and considered all of the important traits.

And I did not find anything better for the body than silence: Rambam, may his memory be blessed, already explained about the matter of silence that if it was about speech that brings damage to a person in every way or that brings gain from one side but damage from the other, Rabban Shimon ben Gamliel would not have needed to warn us about it - as every person who guards himself from anguish would be careful about it. But rather, even with speech that brings no damage to a person at all and is all gain, like one who speaks about his business affairs and the needs of his body and the needs of his livelihood - one must minimize speech and not be long-winded in it, but rather [just speak] according to his need. And it is not necessary to say about a vain matter that does not [change a thing] that one should not mention it at all. And so [too] did they say in Talmud Yerushalmi - "Rabban Shimon ben Gamliel said, If I had been at Mount Sinai, I would have needed two mouths. Afterwards he said, now that we only have one, I am not able to save our souls from evil speech, all the more so if we had two.'" He means to say he wanted two mouths so that he should not speak from his one mouth words of Torah and words that are completely vain things of the world; in the same [way] that our holy sages would make themselves like vessels of [the sacrificial] service, which are not to be used for profane matters. And this is that which we say in the Talmud of the Westerners

Talmud Yerushalmi - "All chatter patatia is bad except for Torah chatter which is good." And some have the version, "All karavia is bad except for Torah karavia which is good." And the meaning of karavia is plowing. This is to say that all of the words and thoughts with which a person makes efforts in this world, it is all vain and bad spirit, besides thoughts about Torah and 'the acts of God, as they are awesome.

And the exposition of Torah is not what is essential, but the action: This is saying that one should not expostulate on a commandment to others while he does not do it himself. Rather, he should do them first and [then] teach them to others - as the rabbis, may their memory be blessed, said - "Pleasant are words that come out of the mouth of one who practices them."

And whoever increases words brings sin. This matter is speaking about words of Torah, as a person should not increase words of law, but rather wait and think out what he will say, such that his words be measured and they not be hasty. As when there are many words, transgression will not be avoided, as he will think the matter is like this and he will bring sin with his mistaken ruling. And hence they said, "And the exposition of Torah is not what is essential, but the action," to make known that that statement is speaking abut words of Torah. And this statement as well should not be explained to be about vanities of the world - as if [had been] so, they should have made it adjacent to "and I did not find anything better for the body than silence," as that is about mundane words. And then immediately it [should] say, "And whoever increases words brings sin." But rather they said it about words of Torah, as we have explained.

18. Rabban Shimon ben Gamaliel used to say: on three things does the world stand: On justice, on truth and on peace, as it is said: "execute the judgment of truth and peace in your gates".

<u>Rabbeinu Yonah</u>

Rabban Shimon ben Gamliel says, On three things the world subsists: on judgment: That he should judge a truthful judgment.

On truth: As a person should walk in the paths of repentance, as He is true and His Torah is true' and walk in the ways of the Holy One, blessed be He, of truth. And he should also go in that path, as it is stated - "and you shall go in His ways." And the sages, may their memory be blessed, said - that even in the recounting of mundane words should a person not lie, like that story of Rav's son, etc.: Rav said to him, "Your mother has improved." He said back to him, "It is I that reversed your words to bring about the change." He said, "This is as people say - **The one that comes from you will teach you reason**. But you should not do this because of that which is stated - "they taught their mouths to speak words of falsehood." For a person who accustoms his tongue to speak falsehood about a matter that has neither a loss nor gain will, when he comes to speak matters of principle, also not be able to speak the truth; as it is his mouth that will speak and habit rules over it.

And on peace: Peace includes all good, things in the world, and there is no end to its benefits. And may there be peace upon Israel.

Chapter 2

1. Rabbi Said: which is the straight path that a man should choose for himself? One which is an honor to the person adopting it, and on account of which honor accrues to him from others. And be careful with a light commandment as with a grave one, for you did know not the reward for the fulfillment of the commandments. Also, reckon the loss that may be sustained through the fulfillment of a commandment against the reward accruing thereby, and the gain that may be obtained through the committing of a transgression against the loss entailed thereby. Apply your mind to three things and you will not come into the clutches of sin: Know what there is above you: an eye that sees, an ear that hears, and all your deeds are written in a book.

Rabbeinu Yonah

Rabbi Yehuda ha'Nasi said: Which is the straight path that a person should choose for himself? Whichever [path] that is itself praiseworthy for the person adopting [it], And praiseworthy to him from other people: When the commandments are done, the Holy One, blessed be He, is made praiseworthy through them and that is true praiseworthiness for people. And therefore, one should choose this path for himself.

And praiseworthy to him from other people: That he does the commandments in their appropriate time, as it is stated - "and how good is a thing in its time." As he can do them in a time that is not right in the eyes of the creatures and it will not attain praiseworthiness from them. And that is not doing

Pirkei Avot - Rabbeinu Yonah - Chapter 2

the complete commandment; as the matter that the sages, may their memory be blessed, said - "Anyone who does a commandment according to its statement nullifies even a decreed judgment of seventy years, as it is stated - Inasmuch as a king's command is authoritative, and none can say to him, "What are you doing?" and it is written after it, one who obeys the commandment will not know evil." He should also beautify the commandments, a beautiful lulav [palm frond], a beautiful Talit [prayer shawl], a beautiful scroll of the Torah, Tefillin and the like, in a manner that people will praise it and complement him about them. And Rambam, may his memory be blessed, explained this Mishnah to be about character traits, to follow the middle path which is the choice path and is praiseworthy for the one that adopts it. As it establishes **a pure heart** in a person and renews a proper spirit in his soul. And "it is praiseworthy to him from other people," in that the creations learn to act well and properly from him. For example - with the trait of generosity, A miser will not be called noble, and also a spendthrift will see evil. And so who is the generous one? One who - even though he loves money and saves it very well - consults generously and orders his spending so that he will have enough 'to do the good and the straight' in the place that is fitting to give to. So too there is no trait under the sun that is proper except besides the middle path. And these traits are praiseworthy for the person adopting it, and praiseworthy to him from other people but not if he does too little or too much.

And be as careful with a light commandment as with a weighty one, for you do not know the reward given for the fulfillment of the respective commandments: Even though the punishments for sins are explained to us - as some of them are with excision [karet] and some with death at the hands of Heaven, excision being that he and his seed are cut off whereas death at the hands of Heaven is only that he is cut off, and there are some sins that get the four death penalties meted out by the court, and there are negative commandments that bring forty lashes, and the one who transgresses the rabbinic laws gets rabbinic lashes for rebellion - but the reward of the positive commandments is not explained to us, not for the light ones and not for the weighty ones. And the sages, may their memory be blessed, demonstrated this with a parable, "To what is this similar? To a king who gave an orchard for his servants in which to plant trees. And if he made known to them the giving of reward of the different trees, they would have all toiled on those trees that have a large reward, and it would come out that the orchard would be missing the other trees. So too, were the Holy One, blessed be He, to make known the giving of reward for the different commandments, people would do the weighty ones that have a large reward and leave over the light ones that have a smaller reward, and a person would be incomplete in the commandments." And for this reason, one should not be lenient about the commandments, and his soul should hold them all dear to do, since he does not know which are the light ones and which are the weighty ones. But our rabbi [Rabbi Yehuda Ha'Nassi, the author of this Mishnah] excelled in his words and gave a stronger reason than this and said that "you do not know the reward given for the fulfillment of the respective commandments" as to how much it is, as even the reward of a light commandment is highly elevated. And you should be careful not to lose such a great gain, like the matter that they said - "If you chance upon the nest of a bird in front of you, etc. - and if for a commandment as light as a small coin the Torah says, in order that it will be good for you, in the world that is completely good, and that you will have length of days in the world that is completely long, all the more is it so for the weighty commandments of the Torah."

Also, weigh the loss that may be sustained through the fulfillment of a commandment against the reward that may be obtained for fulfilling it: As if your heart will whisper something to say, "How will I do this and lose my money with this and that"; you can also say to it, "Because there will be a great reward for it, two thousand times the loss." And with this, it will not prevent you from glory.

And weigh the gain that may be obtained through the committing of a transgression against the loss that may be sustained by committing it: Lest there be in your heart the base thought to say, "There is great reward in doing this sin and I will gain very much with it and I will have great pleasure; and how can I not do it?" - guard yourself and consider that which you will lose from it in the end of days, as it is many times over that which you will gain now. And the future pain is much longer and bigger than the temporary pleasure. And when you put this into your heart, your hand will cease from doing it; as a person does not want a gain that has a greater loss attached to it.

Keep your eye on three things, and you will not come to sin: Know what is above you: An Eye that sees, and an Ear that hears, and all your deeds are written in a book: He means to say that the Holy One, blessed be He, sees and knows all the actions of people and remembers everything as if it is written in front of Him, and He will repay evil for a person's evil deeds. And it is a wonder why he counted them as three things, as the three of them are really one thing. As this is all just saying that God knows everything and will pay back in the future according to the deed. And so, what is this calculation, as they are all one matter? Hence, it appears that the explanation is that this matter is a metaphor: that in the same way that when he is standing in front of kings and in front of ministers and sages and men of repute, he would be embarrassed to do things that are not done and from saying things that are not good; so too should he think at all times as if he is in front of the Holy One, blessed be He, in the same way as a man stands in front of his companion. And with this, he will guard his way - also his mouth and his tongue - from sinning, and from anguish to his soul. And that is why he said, "Know what is above you: An Eye that sees, and an Ear that hears," and counted them as two things - an Eye that sees corresponding to the deed and an Ear that hears corresponding to the speech. And God forbid - it is not a real eye nor a real ear. But rather, he means to say that there is no deed that is hidden from in front of Him nor one that is unknown to Him. And the third thing is "and all your deeds are written in a book" - meaning to say that there is no forgetting in front of His throne of glory. And behold, all things are ordered in front of Him, as if they were written in a book, to pay their doers according to their actions and according to the deeds of their hands in the end of days. And if a person puts into his heart the payback that will be given to him, he will prevent himself from doing sins. And about this, he said, "Keep your eye on these three things and you will not come to sin."

2. Rabban Gamaliel the son of Rabbi Yehuda Ha'nasi said: excellent is the study of the Torah when combined with a worldly occupation, for toil in them both keeps sin out of one's mind; But study of the Torah which is not combined with a worldly occupation, in the end comes to be neglected and becomes the cause of sin. And all who labor with the community, should labor with them for the sake Heaven, for the merit of their forefathers sustains them the community, and the forefather's righteousness endures for ever; And as for you, God in such case says I credit you with a rich reward, as if you yourselves had actually accomplished it all.

Rabbeinu Yonah

Rabban Gamliel the son of Rabbi Yehudah HaNasi said: Excellent is the study of the Torah together with a worldly occupation derekh erets, literally, the way of the world, etc.: He means to say derekh erets as in work. As sometimes, the expression, "derekh erets" is like its simple meaning and sometimes it is said for work - it is all dependent on the context.

For the exertion and expended, in both of them causes sin aavon to be forgotten: This is meaning to say that it removes the evil impulse, as it is stated - "Indeed I was born with iniquity aavon; with sin my mother conceived me." As by that which he exerts himself with Torah study and work, the evil impulse does not rule over him - since the whole time that he is not rich and fat, it is not pleasant for him to do sins. Hence one should be involved in Torah - which saps the strength of a man - and also in his work for the sake of his livelihood. And he should never be idle, lest he indulge 'and his heart becomes haughty, to forget the Lord,' as the matter that is stated - "And Yeshurun will grow fat and kick."

And all study of the Torah in the absence of a worldly occupation comes to nothing in the end: Like the matter that they said in our treatise -"If there is no flour, there is no Torah." The matter is like its simple understanding - when he neglects work, it brings him to poverty and it drags along several sins and its evil is great. As on account of it, he will love gifts and not live, and flatter people even if they are evildoers, in order that they give to him. Also, when the money from the gifts runs out, he will become a thief or a kidnapper or gambler and will bring home loot taken from the poor so that he not dies of hunger. And when a person reaches these traits, his spirit knows no restraint and he will not rest and not be still until he transgresses all of the commandments that are stated in the Torah, since 'one sin brings along [another] sin.' And about this, the sages said in - "Anyone who benefits from his toil, the verse states about him - If you eat the toil of your hands you shall be happy and it will be good for you, happy in this world, and good for you in the world to come. Therefore, it is necessary for a sage to know a craft, as it is stated - "Good is wisdom with an inheritance."

And all who work for the community, let them work for the sake of the name of Heaven: Not to be honored and not to derive benefit from them and not to lord over them, but rather to lead them in the straight path, and everything should be for the name of Heaven.

For the merit of their ancestors sustains them, And their righteousness tsidkatam will endure forever: As even though you are involved with them, their needs are accomplished by them; it is not you that caused them, but rather it is the merit of the ancestors of the community that "sustains them, And their righteousness will endure forever" - for a thousand generations.

And as for you who work for the community, God says: I credit you with a great reward, as if you yourselves had

done it on your own: Even though the merit of their ancestors sustained them and their needs were accomplished by the merit of their ancestors, and not by you, you the ones working - I credit you as if all their needs were accomplished by you and in your merit. So did the early scholars rishonim explain. But there is another explanation that can be given: "And all who work for the community, let them work for the sake of the name of Heaven", and do not say - "Why is this distress to me, to work for the needs of community?" And he will think that even if he does charity, the giving of the reward will only be to the community, as it is their money. Since you should not think this thing, as you will benefit yourself for your sake doubly, since "that the merit of their ancestors sustains them," and you will be more successful in their deeds than you would be able to be successful in your own deeds. And I will credit you with the reward, as if you had done everything from your money and as if you gave that which was given through you from your own pocket. And behold, you are gaining with your toil from their deeds more than you would if you were toiling for yourself, since their deeds are more numerous than your deeds. And 'all that you do, the Lord will make successful in your hand,' since "the merit of their ancestors sustains them." Hence one who works for the community will benefit himself very much - but only if he directs his heart to Heaven.

3. Be careful [in your dealings] with the ruling authorities for they do not befriend a person except for their own needs; they seem like friends when it is to their own interest, but they do not stand by a man in the hour of his distress.

<u>Rabbeinu Yonah</u>

Be careful about the government: Which is to say to distance oneself from the government, as in the end they bring a person down from his assets.

As they approach a man only when they need him: It appears that it needs to say, "And it is not a matter of governance, but rather it is to investigate people; and there is no end to their thoughts, and who can get to their ult plans.

They seem like good friends in good times, but they don't stay for him in time of his trouble: They are friendly when they have a shortage of money, but when desperate they don't have mercy upon the poor person until they bring him down from his assets, and they forget the earlier relations since it is all past and gone. And such is the simple understanding of this mishnah. But if the matter is so, it speaks about the defect of kings. But forbid it, forbid it, that such should be the matter and that it should arise. As through them the whole world is sustained and they create law and justice in the world. And there is no man that can be as truthful as they, as they do not need to flatter creatures since they are not afraid; and so, there is nothing that prevents them from walking the straight path. And hence it appears that it can be said that the kings - be it their friendship or be it their enmity - are not in their own hands. And so, when the king needs a person and brings him close and shows him friendship at the time that he benefits from him, it is from God that the matter went out, and not from the king. And God arranged that this person be of benefit to the king. And when a man sins to God and he is guilty and He wants to press him, who can stand for him?

Pirkei Avot - Rabbeinu Yonah - Chapter 2

And even if the king wants to do him honor, it is only in his hand to surely take the vengeance of God and to afflict the one that the Lord would love to chastise. And this is what it states - "Like channeled water is the heart of the king in the Lord's hand." He wants to say, just like a person can direct a channel to any side that he wants, so too is the heart of the king in the hand of the Lord to direct it to do good to the person whose honor He desires and 'to pay back His enemies in his face to destroy him. And he stated - "the heart of the king" and he was not speaking about other people; but so is it that all hearts are in the hand of the Lord. As even though, a person thinks thoughts and it appears to the eyes that he has the ability in his hand to act; in truth he does not have the power in his hand to do bad or to do good, but rather to do the word of the living God.

4. He used to say: do His will as though it were your will, so that He will do your will as though it were His. Set aside your will in the face of His will, so that he may set aside the will of others for the sake of your will. Hillel said: do not separate yourself from the community. Do not trust in yourself until the day of your death. Do not judge your fellow man until you have reached his place. Do not say something that cannot be understood [trusting] that in the end it will be understood. Say not: when I shall have leisure, I shall study; perhaps you will not have leisure.

Rabbeinu Yonah

He was accustomed to say: Make His God's will like your will: Just as when a person does his own will with want and desire, so should he do the will of the Holy One, blessed be He. And he should not separate between the will of the blessed Holy One, blessed be He, and his own will, but rather make both of them into one thing. He means to say that he should not will anything that is not the will in front of God. And they said in the Fathers According to Rabbi Nathan - "And so did David say - but all is from You, and it is from Your Hand that we have given to You." And he gave a good counsel to people to overcome their nature [and] do the desire and will of God, may He be blessed, also from their money and from the acquisitions: because God gave everything and what they have is only a deposit in their hands. And when [one] brings this up into his heart, at the very least he will do the will of the owners, which is God - with the deposit. And with this, he will not worry when he gives charity and he will do the will of the Holy One, blessed be He, willingly and with a good heart.

So that He will make your will like His will: God, may He blessed, satiates the will of every living thing, and gives bread to all flesh, and to every creature according to it lack and this is His want and His will. And if you merit to find favor in front of Him, He will do your will also with the needs of your small world, and give you your sustenance, which is actually His will for all that come to the world.

Nullify your will to His will: of the Holy One, blessed be He.

So that He will nullify the will of others to your will.

Hillel says: Do not separate yourself from the community: At the time when the community is involved with Torah study and with the commandments, it is the crown of all the worlds and the glory of all of His domain. As with many people that are gathered to fulfill His commandment, it is the King's glory; and so, it is not fitting to separate from them, as it is stated - "And there is a King in Yeshurun with the gathering." And this is with a community that goes in the good path and gathers to do a commandment. But it is not fitting to attach oneself to a community that leans to the bad path and the deeds of which are corrupted. And one who separates from them, behold, he is praiseworthy. And about this Yirmiyahu the prophet, peace be upon him, stated - "Oh, to be in the desert, at an encampment for wayfarers! Oh, to leave my people, to go away from them - for they are all adulterers, a band of rogues".

Do not believe in yourself until the day of your death: This is learned out to be both about piety and about faith, that even though you have been fitted with a faithful and proper spirit, you should not be righteous in your own eyes. And you should not say, "How many days have I not done any iniquity - I have defeated my impulse and I am able to overcome, it - it is beaten, already 'broken, and we have escaped' and it cannot divert me from the straight path." But it is an enemy and seeks to ambush you when it finds you sometimes involved in your work and not studying and not thinking about words of the living God, it will then dance in front of you and speak to your heart to divert you to roam in the earth and to walk in a path that no good man has trodden or sat there. And maybe it can thus overcome you and your soul will be taken in its hand. And so, guard yourself and guard your soul much, and do not distance its fear from you, and act with your wisdom if you are a wise man to always place your eyes and your heart upon its ways, until it not be able to come close to you all the days of your life. And about this is it said, "Do not believe in yourself until the day of your death." Also concerning the matter of faith is this thing said, that you not study from the heretics - and not even true things - as their damage is dangerous, lest the sinners seduce you and you desire their words - as they pull in the heart. "And do not believe in yourself until the day of your death," to say, "I will listen to them." And if you might say, "I will accept the good and the bad I will not accept"; you should not rely upon your intellect, as Rabbi Meir did in his studying in front of Elisha the Other, the heretic. This is found in Tractate - they said about him metaphorically, "he found a pomegranate, he ate the inside, he threw out the peel. However, not all people are the same. As you find Yochanan the High Priest who served in the High Priesthood seventy [eighty] years, and in the end became a Sadducee. As there is a very big punishment for even listening to them speaking words of Torah; and as we say - about that sage that was delivered to the heretics; and they said to him, "Maybe you heard heresy and it gave you pleasure, etc".

Do not judge your fellow until you come to his place: This is also from the topic that a person should not believe in himself and not overly rely on his intellect. And when he sees his fellow in a high position and not act straight, he should not say, "If I would fill his place, I would not do one evil thing from all the evil that he is doing." As you don't know this and you are no different than he as far as being a person - and perhaps the position would sway you as well. Only when you reach his place and his position and forego your weaknesses, then do you have the right to wonder about his weaknesses.

Do not say something that cannot be heard, for in the end it will be heard: As a person must guard and be careful from the possibility. Hence if you have a secret, do not tell it even to someone who is your soulmate. And don't say, "It is impossible that this thing be heard, as there is no stranger among us to transport these words." And in the end, everything is heard. Even between you and yourself, do not make it heard to your ears, as the rabbis, may their memory blessed, metaphorically said - "Do not talk among the walls, for the walls have ears." And about this, Shlomo - peace be upon him said - "for a bird of the air may carry the utterance, And a winged creature may report the word".

Do not say, "When I will be available, I will study [Torah]," lest you never become available: Since you do not know what a new day will bring and they will also call you tomorrow, since they will speak new matters and you will have to follow their paths. As there is no lack of new matters requiring your attention every day. And it will come out that you will leave the world without Torah knowledge. But rather you should 'make your Torah fixed' and your work flexible.

5. He used to say: A brute is not sin-fearing, nor is an ignorant person pious; nor can a timid person learn, nor can an impatient person teach; nor will someone who engages too much in business become wise. In a place where there are no men, strive to be a man.

Rabbeinu Yonah

He was accustomed to say: A boor [Ignoramus] cannot fear sin. An ignorant person [literally, a man of the land - am haarets] cannot be pious: The boor is empty, he does not have in him Torah or commandments or the way of the world in terms of good traits. And in the Targum [translation] - "do not place," is "do not tabur. And he did not need to say, a boor cannot be pious, since he is not even one who fears sin, as from his emptiness, he does not even know to guard himself from sins. But an ignoramus is involved with the creatures through important traits and has a few straight dispositions: He knows how to protect himself and so he guards himself from transgressions. And he is even able to be righteous and to do and to fulfill what he is told that he is commanded. But only one who is great in Torah knowledge can reach the level of piety, since it is a trait that requires purity of heart and cleanness of soul. And [the ignoramus] does not have the wisdom in his hand to veer from the middle marker to the far end, to fulfill going beyond the letter of the law. And because of this he is called an am haarets - since he is with them in derekh erets [good manners], and because most of the world **land haarets** is like him.

A person prone to being ashamed cannot learn: The trait of shame is good in every matter except for study, as the matter is stated - "I will speak of Your testimonies, and not be ashamed in the presence of kings." As when David, peace be upon him, was running away from Shaul and he stood in front of kings of the nations of the world, he was not ashamed of speaking words of Torah and of the commandments - even if they mocked him and ridiculed his words. As shame is not good in study. And also, the student should not say, "How can someone as foolish as I ask something of a great Torah sage, who is so sharp in wisdom, whereas I have neither intelligence nor understanding." If this will be his doctrine all of the day, from where will wisdom come to him? And this is what the sage's masters of wisdom, may their memory be blessed, said in the book, Choice Pearls, "Ask the question of fools, and guard the guardings of the generous." This means to say, just like the generous do not squander their money and do not hoard it, but give it readily and willingly to the places that are fitting - as we have explained above; so too with wisdom, speak about it with fit people at fit times, but not with every person and not at a time when he knows that his words will not be heard. It comes out that you say that it is for them to ask every question and not to be ashamed, so that he will learn the things.

An impatient person cannot teach: It is not needed that a teacher be angry nor that he be short of patience; but rather he should be magnanimous and answer everything that he has that they ask. Even if they have difficulty in understanding his answer, he should review it for them until they come to the depth of the matter.

Not all who engage in a lot of business become wise: Since he is involved in his business all of the day and makes it fixed and his Torah flexible, he will never become wise.

In a place where there is no man, strive to be a man: The early scholars [rishonim] explained, "In a place where there is no man" to help you in the commandments and to chastise you, "strive to be a man" and straighten yourself, so as to only do that which is good and straight in the eyes of the Lord. Another explanation: "In a place where there is no man" - if you see a generation wherein the Torah is slacking, stand up and strive with it, as it is stated - "It is a time to do for the

Pirkei Avot - Rabbeinu Yonah - Chapter 2

Lord, they have abrogated your Torah." What is the reason that "it is a time to do for the Lord?" Because "they have abrogated your Torah" - as its beginning is learned from its end - as it is found at the Talmud. And we can also explain, "In a place where there is no man" greater than you in wisdom, "strive to be a man." And do not refrain from becoming wiser, even if you cannot find a sage greater than you in your city. Even if there is no one like you in that whole generation, see yourself as if you were in the generation of the sages of the Talmud and you are with them in one place. Even if you acquire their level, think as if you are standing with the prophets, up until Moshe, our teacher - peace be upon him. And when will you reach their level and their wisdom? And in this way, you will never slack from learning Torah and you will improve your traits each and every day - as you will add to your wisdom and you will be like a flowing spring.

6. Moreover he saw a skull floating on the face of the water. He said to it: because you drowned others, they drowned you. And in the end, they that drowned you will be drowned.

<u>Rabbeinu Yonah</u>

He also saw a skull that was floating on top of the water: Because you killed and caused the skull of the killed man to float, they killed you and made your skull float. But it was not like the law and it is as if they spilled innocent blood. And that is the case, because it is not in your hand to kill the murderer, but rather it is for the court, according to the laws of the Torah. And anyone else who kills him is obligated the death penalty, since his blood is not delivered into the hand of the killer to kill him. And because of this, in the end, those that drowned you will be drowned by others. They will do to them as they did to others. As this thing will be like this since they are all guilty, and an act engendering guilt is given over to the guilty.

7. He used to say: The more flesh, the more worms; The more property, the more anxiety; The more wives, the more witchcraft; The more female slaves, the more lewdness; The more slaves, the more robbery; [But] the more Torah, the more life; The more sitting [in the company of scholars], the more wisdom; The more counsel, the more understanding; The more charity, the more peace. If one acquires a good name, he has acquired something for himself; If one acquires for himself knowledge of Torah, he has acquired life in the world to come.

Rabbeinu Yonah

He was accustomed to say: The more flesh, etc. A person thinks that he adds life with pleasure and pampering, as he acts according to nature. But there is no control over the day of death, it will not be a help or a benefit, but it will be for shame' and even for vermin.

The more possessions, the more worry: Do not think that because of the honor of his wealth and the multitude of his assets, he will while away his days in bounty and his years in pleasantness. But instead, he will worry about them the whole entire year. Ask him and he will tell you, your wealthy ones and they will say to you.

The more man-servants, the more theft. The more maidservants, the more lewdness. The more wives, the more witchcraft: And if the man-servants steal, he is struck for them - as it is in his hand to stop them. And even if he does not know [about it], the matter will be cast upon him - as they are his money and his gold, they belong to him. Also, when the maidservants are lewd with others, the matter is upon him as if he himself was lewd, as an abomination was done in his house. Also, in the proliferation of wives, he causes them to do witchcraft, to increase love towards them: the hated one will redouble her efforts until she sways his heart, and her rival was surely angered. And they will hang the matter upon his neck, since it is a major sin, as it is stated - "You shall not let a witch live".

The more Torah, the more life: This matter corresponds to that which he said, "The more flesh, the more vermin." As through enjoyment, he will shorten his days; but through toil in Torah study, they will be lengthened. And it also corresponds to - "The more possessions, the more worry," as the worry over possessions shortens his years. But the worry over Torah - even though it is great worry, to the one who understands, when he figures out the law to the point that he can 'say the thing in an apt fashion' - this worry cannot cause him evil. Even though the wise men of science have said that concern is sickness of the heart and worry is destruction of the heart, worry over Torah will increase for him length of days and years of life and peace. And about this Shlomo, peace be upon him, said - "The fear of the Lord adds life; the years of the wicked will be shortened".

The more wisdom, the more sitting and studying: He means to say, the wisdom of reasoning and argument, as through this, he increases sitting. As students will come to hear the new ideas and to sharpen themselves with him and to learn the matter of the novel rationale - as this is a wisdom in of itself. And he means to say that he is given reward corresponding to all of them, since he is the catalyst. And this matter corresponds to that which he said, "The more maidservants, the more lewdness." As there are things that others do and it is seen as if he did it himself, for the bad or for the good.

The more charity, the more peace: Due to benefiting from his money, people love the one who gives charity and he increases peace in the world. And also, when he gives advice to others to give charity, it is considered as if he gave it himself. And people love him for this and also for that. It corresponds to that which he said, "The more man-servants, the more theft." As there, it is because of the actions of others - the theft of his servants - that people hate him. But one who increases charity, which causes others to give, increases his love from the creatures.

One who has acquired a good name has acquired for himself: As the good name for himself, he will not leave to others. It is the opposite of the one who increases possessions, since with his death, he - the one who comes from them' will leave them over and go without desire.

One who has acquired words of Torah, has acquired for himself the life of the World to Come:

8. Rabban Yohanan ben Zakkai received [the oral tradition] from Hillel and Shammai. He used to say: if you have learned much Torah, do not claim credit for yourself, because for such a purpose were you created. Rabban Yohanan ben Zakkai had five disciples and they were these: Rabbi Eliezer ben Hyrcanus, Rabbi Joshua ben Hananiah, Rabbi Yose, the priest, Rabbi Shimon ben Nethaneel and Rabbi Eleazar ben Arach. Rabbi Johanan used to list their outstanding virtues: Rabbi Eliezer ben Hyrcanus is a plastered cistern which loses not a drop; Rabbi Joshua ben Hananiah happy is the woman that gave birth to him; Rabbi Yose, the priest, is a pious man; Rabbi Simeon ben Nethaneel is one that fears sin, And Rabbi Eleazar ben Arach is like a spring that ever gathers force. Rabbi Yohanan used to say: if all the sages of Israel were on one scale of the balance and Rabbi Eliezer ben Hyrcanus on the other scale, he would outweigh them all. Abba Shaul said in his name: if all the sages of Israel were on one scale of the balance, and Rabbi Eliezer ben Hyrcanus also with them, and Rabbi Eleazar ben Arach on the other scale, he would outweigh them all.

<u>Rabbeinu Yonah</u>

Rabban Yochanan ben Zakkai received the tradition from Hillel and Shammai. He used to say: If you have learned a lot of Torah, do not credit it favorably, etc. You are still at the beginning, and when will you reach the middle and the end? As the Torah's measurement is longer than the land and wider than the sea, and human comprehension is not able to reach the far end of it. And how distant is a man from it; and so how can he credit it favorably for himself? And he has not accomplished even one **Torah** from the thousand that he is to accomplish.

Because for this you were created: The Holy One, blessed be He, only brought you into existence to do His will. And also, for this reason is it not for you to credit it favorably for yourself if you have accomplished much Torah - "because for this you were created." There is a metaphor about this: If a debtor repays his debt, do we credit it favorably to him for that? And this measure is also true for the commandments - that if you have done many commandments, "do not credit if favorably for yourself, because for this you were created".

Rabbi Yochanan ben Zakkai had five students: Rabbi Eliezer ben Horkenos, Rabbi Yehoshua ben Chananya, Rabbi Yosi the Priest, Rabbi Shimon ben Netanel, and Rabbi Elazar ben Arakh. He would recount their praises: Rabbi Eliezer ben Horkenos is a pit covered in plaster that does not lose a drop: The explanation is that he did not forget anything ever from all that which he learned, like the pit after it has been plastered with plaster and does not lose a drop, as the water is not absorbed, even by the sides of the pit.

Rabbi Yehoshua ben Chananya - happy is the one who gave birth to him: The undifferentiated expression, **happy** is a category that includes all of the virtues through which a person is happy. And when it mentions the trait with it, it is referring only to a particular trait. And we have found it stated about fear as in "Happy is the man who fears the Lord". And also, about the designation of a fixed place for Torah study, as it is written - "Happy is the man who listens to me, coming early to my gates each day, waiting outside my doors," and it states - "Happy are those who dwell in Your house; they will still forever praise You." And about devotion, as it is stated - "Happy is the man You choose and bring near to dwell in Your courts." And about faith - "Happy is the man who has refuge in You." It is also stated about one who prevents himself from involvement with evildoers -

"Happy is the man who has not followed the counsel of the evildoers, or taken the path of sinners, or joined the company of the scorners." It is also stated about those that keep the Shabbat - "Happy is the man who does this." It is also stated about those that walk in the Torah of the Lord - "Happy are those whose way is blameless, who follow the Torah of the Lord." It is also stated about those that keep the commandments - "Happy are those who observe His decrees, who turn to Him wholeheartedly." It is also stated about one who benefits from his toil - "You shall enjoy the fruit of your labors; you shall be happy and it shall be good for you." It is also stated about those that keep the law and do justice - "Happy are those who act lawfully, who do justice at all times." It is also stated about trust in God - "he who trusts in the Lord is happy." It is also stated about wisdom - "Happy is the man who finds wisdom," and it is also written - "he who shows pity for the lowly is happy." And about this is it said, "happy is the one who gave birth to him" undifferentiated; meaning to say he is happy with all of the happy traits - great in his wisdom and refined by his traits and in all of his affairs.

Rabbi Yosi the Priest is pious: As in all of his deeds, he would do beyond the letter of the law. And about this is it said in many places in the Talmud - "we have learned the trait of piety here".

Rabbi Shimon ben Netanel fears sin: As he would make fences to distance himself from the sins.

And Rabbi Elazar ben Arakh is an ever-strengthening fountain: As he was very sharp and a logician and innovate ideas from his intellect.

He - Rabban Yochanan ben Zakkai used to say: If all the sages of Israel were on one side of a balance scale, etc.: He means to say concerning knowledge. As he was like a plastered pit that does not lose a drop, and there was none among the sages of Israel that knew as much as he, who would not forget a thing from all that he learned.

Abba Shaul said in his name that if all the sages of Israel, including Rabbi Eliezer ben Horkenos, were on one side of a balance scale, and Rabbi Elazar ben Arakh were on the other side, he - Rabbi Elazar would outweigh them all: Concerning sharpness and logic did he praise Rabbi Elazar ben Arakh over all of the sages of Israel. It comes out that you will say that these two teachers [the Tannaim] do not disagree, but rather here it is speaking about logic and sharpness.

9. He - Rabban Yohanan said unto them: go forth and observe which is the right way to which a man should cleave? Rabbi Eliezer said, a good eye; Rabbi Joshua said, a good companion; Rabbi Yose said, a good neighbor; Rabbi Shimon said, foresight. Rabbi Elazar said, a good heart. He - Rabban Yohanan said to them: I prefer the words of Elazar ben Arach, for in his words your words are included. He - Rabban Yohanan said unto them: go forth and observe which is the evil way which a man should shun? Rabbi Eliezer said, an evil eye; Rabbi Joshua said, an evil companion; Rabbi Yose said, an evil neighbor; Rabbi Shimon said, one who borrows and does not repay for he that borrows from man is as one who borrows from God, blessed be He, as it is said, "the wicked borrow and do not repay, but the righteous deal graciously and give". Rabbi Elazar said, an evil heart. He - Rabban Yohanan said to them: I prefer the words of Elazar ben Arach, for in his words your words are included.

<u>Rabbeinu Yonah</u>

He said to them: Rabban Yochanan ben Zakkai to his students.

Go out and see what is a straight path that a person should cling to. Rabbi Eliezer says: A good eye: One who is glad about his portion.

Rabbi Yehoshua says: A good friend: That a man cling to a good friend.

Rabbi Yosi says: A good neighbor: To seek good neighbors, since their friendship is constant; and when they are good, their benefit is great. So did the early scholars [rishonim], may their memory be blessed, explain. But it is not the straight path, as according to their words, a good eye and a good heart are things about himself and a good friend and a good neighbor are about others. Hence, we need to explain this mishnah, each word as is fit:

What is a straight path that a person should cling to: From all of the good and straight paths that a person should cling to. He means to say to cling to one trait, to be complete with it. As it is better for a person to grab one trait in full - that it become easy for him to reach all of the important traits via it - than his being someone with attempted mastery of many traits and he is not complete in any one of them. And this is that which Rabbi Eliezer said, A good eye: He means to say the trait of generosity, which is a fine and praiseworthy trait. And once he is at the peak of generosity, he will certainly reach the other virtues - as this trait comes to him because of a broad heart and a good eye. And a person like this is fit for every good trait, and this is what is written, "he who shows pity [mechonen] for the lowly is happy." This means to say that the humble are the ones that find favor in his eyes and so he gives to them with a good eye. This is like the usage - "and they will cherish [mechonen] its dust" - that the dust of the Land of Israel will find favor in their eyes.

Rabbi Yehoshua says: A good friend: That he clings to this straight path and it become easy for him to do it; and to be a good friend to the man that his heart desires, and to accustom himself that another spirit be pleased from him. And thus, he will come to be on friendly terms with all of the creatures.

Rabbi Yosi says: A good neighbor: That he himself be a good neighbor to all of his neighbors. And once he becomes good and a loyal friend to five or eight people, the matter is close for him to love all that come to the world. And so, he is happy and with all of the good traits.

Rabbi Shimon says: Seeing the consequences of one's actions: That he places his eyes on everything, and see all of the things that will be generated before they are generated. And when he sees something that has reward at its beginning but its end will bring a loss, he will distance himself from it. And with this, he will never sin - as he will weigh the gain, that may be obtained through the committing, of a transgression against the loss that may be sustained by committing it. And hence a person should cling to this path to weigh at the beginning that which will be at the end, and to weigh all of his affairs with this approach.

Rabbi Elazar says: A good heart: Rambam, may his memory be blessed, explained that this is the virtue of perfecting the traits - as the attributes of a person come from the heart. And when his heart is good, all of his traits will be straight and all of his attributes will be correct. And he will be glad in his heart, befriend the good and only desire a thing which has a positive goal and not a loss. So did Rabbi Meir Halevi, may his memory be blessed, write. And though the matter is like this, it only follows according to their approach. But this explanation does not fit according to our approach. Hence it appears correct to explain that with "a good heart," he means to say the trait of willpower [literally, will]. That is the tolerant one who is not short tempered, distances himself from the trait of anger and answers softly. Even when someone does evil to him, he tolerates him and there is no bitterness in his mouth - as his palate is sweets and he is all delights.

He said to them: I see the words of Rabbi Elazar ben Arakh as better than. all of yours, because your words are included in his: As a man that has a trait like this dwell within him is also good to his friends and to his neighbors and to the whole world. He also has the trait of generosity; as he is generous to people with his body and heart, to wish what they desire and to do their will, all the more so will he be generous to them with his money. And every good trait will reside in a person like this, as the will of a healthy heart is a greater thing than the act. As behold, the commandments are the action of the limbs and are only labor, and easy to do. But that he should place his eyes and his heart there all the days to think of thoughts to do the labor of God from great devotion and love of God for his Name, may He be blessed - that is the true effort from this thing.

He said to them: Go out and see what is an evil path that a person should distance himself from. Rabbi Eliezer says: A bad eye: We need to explain his question and their answer, as it is a known thing that the opposite of the straight way is the way that a person should distance from himself. And the correct reason that the question was asked is because there are several good traits the opposite of which are not bad; like the trait of piety which is a very great virtue - but if one is not pious, no bad will happen. About this, he said "a bad eye" - meaning to say, that a person not say stinginess is not bad since he doesn't extort or rob from his fellow. But actually, its evil is great, as it is the basis for every bad trait. And from it, he will do every evil thing. As he should not say about this, "If I do not reach the final culmination of the virtues, I will not be a pious man, but I will still be righteous in doing that which I was commanded about." And he does not know that it is 'a lack that cannot be counted.' Yet it will be lacking in his heart at the end of days - as the little that is lacking will be a big lack, as Shlomo, peace be upon him, stated in his wisdom - "Dead flies turn the perfumer's ointment fetid and putrid; so, a little folly outweighs massive wisdom." He meant to say [that] just like a fly - which is a small thing - completely destroys a very important thing, the perfumer's ointment; so too is a little foolishness to the glory of a sage and an honored man. As the trait of miserliness causes a man to be empty [beliaal] of the good traits. It is like we find with Naval the Carmelite: Because he said - "Should I take my bread and my water, etc.," it stated about him - "Please, my lord, pay no attention to that empty man, Naval".

Rabbi Yehoshua says: A bad friend. Rabbi Yosi says: A bad neighbor: In he himself being bad to his friend or his neighbors.

Rabbi Shimon says: One who borrows but does not repay: He could not have said the opposite of "the one who sees the consequences of one's actions" in general is the one from which everyone should distance himself. As everyone distances themselves from this trait on their own. But one is able to cling to it through an action; and so, he took something about which a person should see the consequences in action: One who does not see it does not distance himself from the bad path, like the borrower who does not pay. Since at the time that he borrowed, he should have thought and seen if he would be able to pay up when the time of payment would come. And if he is not aware on his own if he will have the wherewithal in his hand to pay, he should not borrow now - in view of the duress that he will have. Rather, he should endure the current duress, even if he very much needs the loan.

Borrowing from a person is like borrowing from the Omnipresent blessed be He: As we find loaning with the Holy One, blessed be He, as it is stated - "He who has compassion for the poor makes a loan to the Lord; He will repay him his due." It wanted to say that it is as if this compassionate one towards the poor is lending to God, and so he has a great reward. And this is what it says here, "is like borrowing from the Omnipresent" - meaning to say that he not thinks that since I don't have with what to pay and I was already brought to court and they did not find anything for me to pawn and I left innocent, what is my transgression and what is my sin? And the matter to you is as if you borrowed from the Omnipresent, blessed be He; and if you are exempt from the laws of man, you are nonetheless not exempt from the laws of Heaven. And you will not be exempt on account of people as the case will be between you and God. Since when you have a case for a loan with people, you are not exempt - even if people have exempted you. What is the reason? As it is stated - "The evildoer borrows and does not repay; the righteous has compassion and gives", meaning to say, that since he borrowed and does not repay, he is an evildoer. And this is so even though he doesn't have with what to pay, as it was up to him to investigate with what he would repay from the beginning. But the righteous one is compassionate and gives what he has to give, giving it so that he can still repay. Since he is nonetheless careful from the beginning with that with which he can repay. And even though we do not hold it as a credit for the man who repays his obligation; for the righteous one who has grace on his lips in his way in the world, we hold it as a credit when he returns people's money and they become his friends on account of their money.

Rabbi Elazar says: A bad heart. He said to them: I see the words of Rabbi Elazar ben Arakh as better than all of yours, for your words are included in his.

10. They [each] said three things: Rabbi Eliezer said: Let the honor of your friend be as dear to you as your own; And be not easily provoked to anger; And repent one day before your death. And [he also said:] warm yourself before the fire of the wise, but beware of being singed by their glowing coals, for their bite is the bite of a fox, and their sting is the sting of a scorpion, and their hiss is the hiss of a serpent, and all their words are like coals of fire.

Rabbeinu Yonah

They said: The students of Rabban Yochanan ben Zakkai.

Three things: They said many, many things. But rather it wants to say that each one was accustomed to saying three things everyday - like the matter that they said - "It is a pearl in the mouth of Rav" - about things that are always needed.

Rabbi Eliezer says: The honor of your friend should be as dear to you as your own: We have learned the laws of the way of the world [Derekh Erets] here: He should seek the honor of his friend and desire that they honor him, as he desired his own honor. And this is the way of ethics.

And do not be easy to anger: It is known that the trait of anger is very bad, however it is the nature of people to be pulled in by it. Hence, he said that perforce sometimes be careful of anger, so that you not be easy to anger - since your will desire anger: Weigh in the scales of your intellect if this thing is fit to get angry about. And if you find any argument to remove your anger, use it and negate it. But if it is a thing that is fit to be angry about regardless, then your anger will be with you, you can allow yourself to get angry. And this is what Shlomo peace be upon him stated - "Don't let your spirit be quickly angered, for anger rests in the laps of fools"

Pirkei Avot - Rabbeinu Yonah - Chapter 2

- he meant to say, do not be quick to anger, but rather with deliberation and only for a great need. And do not do like the fool, who - because anger resides in his lap - hurries to get angry and does not know to subdue his spirit. And he does this even with something that he does not need anger for; even though he knows that he will spoil the matter as a result of his anger, he will nonetheless not restrain his spirit. He is like the snake which, according to some of the sages - has venom in its teeth, and so when he bites, the venom goes out automatically and the snake does not need to discharge it. So too is anger in the lap of the fools - it is found there and goes out automatically. And this is what the sages, may their memory be blessed, said - "By three things is a person known: his cup, his wallet and his anger".

And repent one day before your death: One should repent today, lest he die tomorrow. And since he does not know the day of his death, it comes out that all of his days will be in repentance. And this is that which is stated - "At all times, let your clothes be white." These three things are a pearl in the mouth of Rabbi Eliezer ben Horkenos, as they are things that are always needed by every man.

And warm yourself by [Keneged] the fire of the sages: The explanation of keneged, here is close to.

But be cautious around their coals that you should not be burned: It is a metaphor of the one that warms himself by the fire: If he stands far from it as is fit for him, it comes out that he benefits and is not burned. But if he approaches too closely, it comes out that he gets burned. So is it with the one who warms himself by the fire of the sages and benefits from their wisdom, he must stand in front of them with awe, fear and seriousness of mind. And he should not act lightheadedly in front of them. And he should not approach them more than they have brought him close, as this trait pushes him away and makes him liable for a big punishment. And it is not necessary to say that this is the case at the time when the sages, stumble in a matter of sin.

For their bite is the bite of a snake, and their sting is the sting of a scorpion: And lest it come into your mind that you can seduce him in the same way that we whisper to charm the snake and he does not bite; the matter is not like that. Rather their bite is the bite of a snake, but their whisper is the whisper of a viper that does not listen to the voice of whisperers [Charmers].

And all of their words are like burning coals: but the matter is understood. And to say "I also have a living spirit and I will make arguments like him." But you should be concerned that the wisdom is not in your hand, lest you are mistaken in your argument. As their words are chosen and there is sharpness in their biting wisdom that is inside of them. And this thing is not from the three things that are counted that Rabbi Eliezer said, as he did not say it every day. And one time that he places into his heart to be careful about the honor of the sages is enough for him for a long time; as it is not something that needs reminding every day, like the first three.

11. Rabbi Joshua said: an evil eye, the evil inclination, and hatred for humankind put a person out of the world.

Rabbeinu Yonah

Rabbi Yehoshua says: The evil eye: Its explanation is one who is not happy with his lot and places his eye on his fellow who is wealthier than he, thinking when will I be as wealthy as the great wealth of this man? And this causes evil to himself and to his fellow. It is like the wise men of science say about everything that is his neighbors: vapor comes up from that thought and burns the things that he put his eye towards with an evil eye. He also burns himself inside. Since he desires things, the thought of which he does not have the ability in his hand to materialize his, he destroys his body - as he shortens his spirit and removes it from the world. And this is the evil eye about which Rabbi Yehoshua spoke. And the proof of this explanation is that here he said, evil eye [Ra] in the masculine - which is the one that put his eye to something for evil. And above, it said evil eye in the feminine [Raah], the explanation of which is about the trait of stinginess. And it is not like the words of some of the commentators. And the evil inclination, and hatred of the creations, like their simple meaning, remove a person from the world.

12. Rabbi Yose said: Let the property of your fellow be as precious unto you as your own; Make yourself fit to study Torah for it will not be yours by inheritance; And let all your actions be for [the sake of] the name of heaven.

Rabbeinu Yonah

Rabbi Yosi says: The money of your friend should be as dear to you as your own: To fulfill the command of its owner.

Prepare yourself to study Torah: Prepare yourself with good traits so that you can study the Torah and reach the level of piety, as it stated - "An ignorant person cannot be pious." And this is what Shlomo, peace be upon him, stated - "Wise things are too lofty for a fool; he does not open his mouth in the gate." He wanted to say that for the fool wisdom is far and very high, who can find it. And in the place where they determine the law and speak with wisdom, he muzzles his mouth, as he does not know what to answer. "He who has thoughts to do harm is called by men a master of plots" - that you not say, it is because the fool's intellect is not directed, that he is not wise; since he does not have the reasoning to know wisdom. As behold, he has thoughts to do harm and his reasoning is great and sharp to do evil to the point that he is nicknamed and they call him, "the master of plots." Rather the wisdom of Torah does not rest upon him because of the evil of his heart - as he has the vessel mind with which to receive it. Also included in "Prepare yourself to study Torah" is to minimize pleasures, so that he learns much Torah, as we have learned - "This is the way to toil in Torah: eat bread with salt, and drink a small amount of water, and sleep on the ground, and live a life whose conditions will cause you pain, and in Torah you toil." As one who increases luxuries will not have wisdom dwell within him - as they said, his neck is fat' his calf is wide.

For it is not an inheritance for you: And you will not acquire it if you do not exert yourself upon it. As it is not like an inheritance from the fathers, in which a child gets it without effort. And even if your fathers were sages or luminaries for several generations, don't think and say [that] the Torah will return to its accustomed guesthouse without any effort. And is the fruit of a righteous one a tree of life. And the matter is not like this, but rather it is only to those that hold on to it and its supporters that are happy. And the wisdom was only given to your fathers and you will not inherit them. And if you desire it, acquire it for yourself with the toil of your hands. And if you do that, you will be happy and it will be good for you.

All of your actions should be for the sake of Heaven: Even optional things like eating, drinking, sitting, getting up, walking, laying down, sexual relations, speech and all the needs of your body should all be for the service of your Creator or for something that leads to His service. How is it with eating and drinking? There is no need to say that he not eats forbidden things; but even if he ate and drank permissible things because he was hungry or thirsty - if he did this for the pleasure of his body, it is not praiseworthy unless he intended to fulfill the needs of his body and to eat in order to live to serve his Creator. Gluttonous eating will also do great evil; as the wise men of science have said that most illnesses are caused as the result of too much food and that a man should only eat to remove his hunger. And through this, he will guard his soul from distress and cause his body to be in good health. But he should not eat every time it is sweet to his palate, as the palate always desires to eat until his stomach is full - according to what a man can fill it. And through this, he will have every illness and ailment, and this is that which is stated - "The righteous man eats to satisfaction, but the belly of the wicked is lacking." As the stomach is only able to digest what it can hold; and when one eats and fills it until the palate no longer desires to eat, he makes the belly lack and destroys it - as the destruction of the belly is it's lack. But the righteous person who eats to the satisfaction of his soul and only to remove his hunger, he sustains the body which the soul loves in order to do the good and the straight in the eyes of the Lord. And the enlightened ones will understand. How is it [with] sitting, getting up and walking? There is no need to say that he not sits in a gathering of scorners and not stand in a place of sinners and not walk in the counsel of evildoers, but even to sit in the council of the straight and to stand in the path of the righteous and to walk in the path of the innocent - if he did it for his own benefit and to fulfill the wants of his body and its desires, it is not praiseworthy; but rather only if he did it for the sake of Heaven. How is it with laying down? There is no need to say that at a time that he can be involved in Torah study and in the commandments and instead arouses himself to sleep to enjoy himself, that it is not fit to do so. But even at a time when he is weary and needs to sleep in order to rest from his weariness - if he does it for the benefit of his body, it is not praiseworthy; but rather only if it is to fulfill the needs of his body in order that he be able to serve his Creator and to give sleep to his eyes and rest to his body, for the needs of health and that his mind not break down in Torah study from the weariness. With sexual relations, there is no need to say that he not commits a sin. But even at the appointed time stated in the Torah, if he does it for the sake of the benefit to his body or to achieve his desire - behold, this is disgraceful. But even if he intended it so that he have sons that will serve him and fill his place, it is not praiseworthy; but rather only if it is that he have sons to serve the Omnipresent, may He be blessed, or that he intended to have sexual relations to fulfill the appointed time stated in the Torah - like who one pays off a debt to his creditor. How is it with speaking? There is no need to say not to recount evil speech and foulness of the mouth and similar to them. But even in recounting words of wisdom, his intention needs to be for the service of his Creator or for something that will bring him to His service. The principle of the matter is that a person is obligated to put his eyes and his heart to his ways, and to weigh all of his deeds in the scales of his mind. And when he sees that something brings him to the service of his Creator, may He be blessed, he should do it; and if not, he should separate from it. And so, wrote Rambam, may his memory be blessed.

13. Rabbi Shimon said: Be careful with the reading of Shema and the prayer. And when you pray, do not make your prayer something automatic, but a plea for compassion before God, for it is said: "for he is gracious and compassionate, slow to anger, abounding in kindness, and renouncing punishment"; And be not wicked in your own esteem.

Rabbeinu Yonah

Rabbi Shimon says: Be careful in the reciting of Shema: Be careful with the reciting of the Shema more than with prayer. This is because the time of the morning prayer is large and wide, as it is up to four hours from daybreak; but the time of reciting Shema in the morning is short and precise - with the sunrise, according to the vatikin [Punctilious Ones]. And this is the reason for the expression, **be careful** - as it requires great care.

When you pray, do not make your prayer fixed, rather prayers for mercy and supplication before the Omnipresent, blessed be He: That he says the prayer like a poor man, supplicating and asking for something that he needs - as a pauper will speak supplications. And he should not be like a man who requests something but does not need it - as he will not supplicate with a full heart, nor with a broken spirit. And every man needs to request about himself, as there is no man in the world who will not sin. And the prayer should also not be like a burden, and he should not do it like one who repays his debt - as it is stated - "You are a compassionate and gracious God, slow to anger, abounding in kindness, renouncing the bad" as every man needs mercy. And if times are fortuitous for him because God, may He be blessed, is slow to anger and forgiving towards him; it is not because of his righteous deeds that God is merciful towards him. And so, he needs to supplicate Him lest God renounce his renouncing of the bad - lest that be caused by sin. And not each and every hour does a miracle occur.

And do not be wicked in your own eyes: That he not be an evildoer in his own eyes, such that he not be able to repent. As it comes out that this one gives up on repentance - and if a sin comes to his hand, it is as if it is permitted to him, since it comes to his mind that it is light compared to the heavy ones that he has transgressed. And he should also not be righteous in his own eyes, as they said Talmud - "The embryo is made to swear in the womb of his mother: Even if the entire world says that you are righteous, be like an evildoer in your own eyes" - and not an actual evildoer, but rather he should be half guilty and half meritorious in his own eyes. If he did one more commandment, happy is he - as he has determined that he be on the side of merit; if he did one more sin, woe to him - as he has determined himself to be on the side of guilt. And this is that which they said in Talmud - "A man should always see himself as if he is half meritorious and half guilty, as it is stated - A wise man is afraid and evades evil." He wanted to say that even though he has evaded evil, the wise man is afraid because he is evil in his own eyes. And it comes out that he runs after the commandments, so that they determine him to be on the side of merit. And he runs from the sins, so that they not determine him to be on the side of guilt.

14. Rabbi Elazar said: Be diligent in the study of the Torah; And know how to answer an epicuros, and know before whom you toil, and that your employer is faithful, for He will pay you the reward of your labor.

Rabbeinu Yonah

Rabbi Elazar says: Be diligent in learning Torah, and know what to respond to one who denigrates the Torah [apikoros]: That one dedicate oneself to study Torah, so that he will know what to respond to the **apikoros**. As if he will not respond to him according to his arguments and his lies, the world will learn from them and drink evil waters - in their seeing that he is defeated, and it will come out that the name of Heaven will be profaned. And an **apikoros** here is one who denies the oral Torah, as well as those that issue rulings not in accordance with the law [Halakha]. And **apikoros** is from the word **Hefker** [chaos; literally, ownerless].

Know before Whom you labor: Before the One who examines the kidneys and the heart. And when you study Torah, exert yourself and put your concentration into it, and that way you will know to respond to the **apikoros** from it. And when you exert yourself in the Torah, delight in it. As we find that the Torah stated - "The Lord created me at the beginning of His course, as the first of His works of old" and it is written after it - "I was a caretaker with it, a delight for me every day." You should behold that the Holy One, blessed be He, would delight in it, and you should do so as well. This is as it is stated - "Rejoicing in His inhabited world, and delighting with mankind." He meant to say that just like the Torah was a delight for the Holy One, blessed be He, before the formation of the world, so too should it be the rejoicing of the habitation and a delight for people after the world was created.

Pirkei Avot - Rabbeinu Yonah - Chapter 2

The Master of your work is trustworthy to pay you the wage for your activity: That you not make your labor in Torah fraudulent, since God, may He be blessed, is the Master of your work and there is nothing hidden from in front of His eyes. And also, since how is it that you would not strain yourself on it, as behold you will have a great wage for your activity? And even thought they said - "Do not be as servants who are serving the master in order to receive a reward"; it is in order to overcome the impulse that sways one form doing the commandments and from walking in the straight path. Hence it is good to think that he will have a reward for them, so that he not gives an opening to the impulse to attack. And also, because they did not warn to know this in order to serve the Omnipresent, may He be blessed - because of the reason of reward. But rather in the same way as a person is obligated to investigate and know the unity of the Omnipresent and His understanding and His wonders that He has done in order to add to His love; so too is he obligated to know that He pays the wage of his activity, to bring up to his heart the greatness of the kindnesses of the Omnipresent - that even though He is the Master of all the creations and the Maker of all and we are all His servants to serve Him and service Him like a slave that is His property without giving a wage, He nonetheless gives that the reward and wage be with us. And on top of everything, we will increase our love from this and we will serve Him with fear and love.

15. Rabbi Tarfon said: the day is short, and the work is plentiful, and the laborers are indolent, and the reward is great, and the master of the house is insistent.

Rabbeinu Yonah

Rabbi Tarfon said, the day is short and the work is great: The day is short, these are a person's days, which are short compared to the Torah, as it is greater. Its measure is longer than the earth and it is wider than the sea, and none can reach down to its end. And this is what they said - those forty days that our teacher Moshe, peace be upon him, stood at Mount Sinai, he did not sleep. There is a parable relevant to this, about] a king that said to his servant, "Measure gold coins from now until tomorrow, and everything that you measure will be yours." How can he sleep, and will he not lose very much at that time? So [too] did Moshe say, "If I sleep, how many pearls of words of Torah will I lose?" All the more so us, that we should not give sleep to our eyes nor slumber to our eyelids.

The workers are lazy and the reward is great: These are people that are lazy in their study of Torah; as even the alacritous sages show laziness. Since it is in the nature of a person to show laziness and no one escapes from it, some do more and some do less.

And the Master of the house is pressing: The One who controls His world that commanded about it. And you are not like a worker who works on consignment. If he does a little, he is given a small wage and if does much, he is given a large wage - according to the calculation that was agreed for him with the entire job. And in this arrangement, the masters are not exacting. But rather the Holy One, blessed be He, commands you the work of the Torah, and the work is not made dependent on you according to all that you are able to do. But rather, if you transgress His command, you will be punished with a big punishment - as you do not have a right to desist from it even one minute.

16. He [Rabbi Tarfon] used to say: It is not your duty to finish the work, but neither are you at liberty to neglect it; If you have studied much Torah, you shall be given much reward. Faithful is your employer to pay you the reward of your labor; And know that the grant of reward unto the righteous is in the age to come.

Rabbeinu Yonah

He used to say: It is not your responsibility to finish the work. That it not come to your mind, "I am not broad hearted and I cannot finish it, and so what advantage is there in toil and what will my exertion benefit." As "it is not your responsibility to finish it." Rather since you are toiling in the Torah, you have fulfilled the commandment of your Creator.

But neither are you free to desist from it: That you not say, "Since I am not obligated to finish the work, I will not pain myself, but rather I will study one hour each day." The matter is not like this, as you are an acquired slave to the work to meditate over it day and night, and then you will make your paths successful and then you will be enlightened.

If you have learned much Torah, your reward will be much: To say that there is an advantage to the one who decides for himself to learn much, as he becomes wiser than the one who learns little - even though both of them do not desist.

And the Master of your work is trustworthy. That you should not fear like a worker, and that the master of the house not say to you, "Go, go and come back," since he doesn't have money in his hand. As you are working for One who will pay you the wage for your activity and pays with trustworthiness.

And know, the giving of reward to the righteous is in the

future to come. And if you think about this, your hand will be strengthened to study the Torah, the measure of which is longer than the earth and it is wider than the sea, and none can reach down to its end to do His commandments. From this you will put upon your heart the greatness of the kindnesses of the Holy One, blessed be He, and you will increase your love for Him.

Chapter 3

1. Akabyah ben Mahalalel said: mark well three things and you will not come into the power of sin: Know from where you come, and where you are going, and before whom you are destined to give an account and reckoning. From where do you come? From a putrid drop. Where are you going? To a place of dust, of worm and of maggot. Before whom you are destined to give an account and reckoning? Before the King of the kings of kings, the Holy One, blessed be he.

Rabbeinu Yonah

Akavia ben Mahalalel says: Keep your eye on three things, and you will not come to sin: Know from where you came: And when you are keeping your eye on where you came from, the thought will cause you to be of a lowly spirit and you will be saved from the trait of arrogance - as it is stated about it - "Every haughty person is an abomination to the Lord".

And to where are you going? To a place of dust, worms, and maggots: And if you think in your heart to where you are going, you will not desire any of the pleasures - as you are toiling for worms. You will also find vain all wealth and honor - 'as it is all vanity and bad spirit.' And about this matter King Shlomo created the Book of Kohelet Ecclesiastes and began - "Vanity of vanities" to show the vanity of all goods and of all honor. And after he showed the vanity of everything, he stated - "The sum of the matter, when all is heard; revere God and observe His commandments; as this is all of man".

Pirkei Avot - Rabbeinu Yonah - Chapter 3

And before Whom are you destined to give an account and a reckoning: As the creations were only created to fear God. As how will a person sin if he thinks in front of Whom he is "destined to give an account and a reckoning", and more than for the punishment and the challenge, as he will suffer great embarrassment. There is a parable [relevant to this] about a king in front of which a man enters: If [the king] finds him cheating in his deeds or lying in his words, he will suffer great embarrassment. All the more so before the King of kings, the Holy One, blessed be He. Also, because the embarrassment of the soul is greater after it separates from the body than the embarrassment when it is still there. As it is the nature of the body to forget, and when a person does an ugly thing and is embarrassed from other people about it for a year or two, he will forget the thing and the embarrassment will leave on its own. Even if it is not forgotten from his heart, the thing will be faded and some of the embarrassment will be removed. As the nature of the body's forgetting mixes with the nature of the soul. And even though it does not overcome it to completely forget the thing, nonetheless it overcomes it enough for the thing to fade; such that some forgetting removes most of the embarrassment. But when the soul is alone, there is no forgetting before it - as it is completely whole and pure and there is no physical nature within it. And when it is embarrassed before "the King of kings, the Holy One, blessed be He," it is for ever and ever that it will stand with the embarrassment like now when it is [actually] standing in front of Him. And like that time, it will stand embarrassed forever. And this is what the rabbis, may there memory be blessed, said - "Woe for this embarrassment, woe for this disgrace." Hence in all cases, the one that raises these things to his heart will not come to sin.

Pirkei Avot - Rabbeinu Yonah - Chapter 3

2. Rabbi Hanina, the vice-high priest said: pray for the welfare of the government, for were it not for the fear it inspires, every man would swallow his neighbor alive. Rabbi Hananiah ben Teradion said: if two sit together and there are no words of Torah spoken between them, then this is a session of scorners, as it is said - "Nor sat he in the seat of the scornful rather, the teaching of the Lord is his delight"; but if two sit together and there are words of Torah spoken between them, then the Shekhinah abides among them, as it is said - "Then they that feared the Lord spoke one with another; and the Lord hearkened and heard, and a book of remembrance was written before Him, for them that feared the Lord and that thought upon His name". Now I have no scriptural proof for the presence of the Shekhinah except among two, how do we know that even one who sits and studies Torah the Holy One, blessed be He, fixes his reward? As it is said - "though he sit alone and meditate in stillness, yet he takes a reward unto himself".

Rabbeinu Yonah

Rabbi Chanina, the Deputy High Priest, says: Pray for the welfare of the government, for were it not for the fear of it: As it is harsh upon us.

Man would swallow his fellow alive: This matter is wanting to say that a person should pray for the peace of the whole world and be in pain about the pain of others. And this is the way of the righteous ones, as David, peace be upon him, stated - "As for me, when they were ill, my dress was sackcloth, I afflicted myself in fasting." As a person should not make his supplications and his requests for his needs alone, but rather to pray for all people, that they be at peace. As with the welfare of the government, there is peace in the world.

Rabbi Chananya ben Teradyon says: Two who are sitting together and there are no words of Torah spoken between them, this is a session of scorners, as it is said - "Happy is the man who has... not sat in the session of the scorners": Two things are called scorning [leitsanut]. One is evil speech: one who speaks badly about his fellow, to disgrace him and to debase him among people, that he be considered scornful in their eyes. And this is from the great sins that a man commits and is guilty. And this trait is only found among those that act wickedly. And about it Shlomo, peace be upon him, stated in his wisdom - "The malevolent, conceited man scorner is his name acts in a frenzy of malevolence." He meant to say that these two evil traits, malevolence and conceit - both them or are included in the scorner. And a malevolent man is one who speaks about his fellow and debases him in the eyes of the world; whereas conceit is in thought, such that another person is not thought of as anything in front of him. And one **crowned** with these two things his name is scorner. And lest you say, he may not watch his tongue, but his hands are tied, he does not sin with them; about this he said, "he acts in a frenzy of malevolence" - when this man that "scorner is his name" comes to action, it will be with anger and cruelty. This is because scorning indicates about him the sin of being one who commits evil deeds. And Shlomo, peace be upon him, would console those that hear the insult of the scorners but do not respond and stated - "At scorners He scorns, but to the lowly He shows grace." He meant to say that God scorns those that scorn you and they will lose more with their scorn than you - the listener. "But to the lowly" that are silent and endure them and don't respond, the Holy One, blessed be He, "shows grace." But the verse that he [Cited in the mishnah], "not sat in the session of the scorners," is not speaking about the scorners that we discussed - as that is already either in the category of sinners or in the category of evildoers that are stated in the beginning of the verse. Rather, it called "the session of the scorners" the opposite of what is written after it: "Rather, in the Torah of the Lord is his desire, and he meditates upon His Torah day and night. That is those that purposely establish sessions to speak about empty words, and forsake words of Torah. As they remove the yoke of Torah from upon them, since during the time that they don't have work and they also don't have to speak about their affairs, they establish a session for their idle words - hence it is called a session of scorners. And this thing is spoken concerning the refraining from Torah study, since this chapter is speaking about the topic of refraining from Torah study.

But two who are sitting together and there are words of Torah spoken between them, the Divine Presence rests with them, as it is said - "Then those who feared the Lord spoke one with another, and the Lord hearkened and heard, and a book of remembrance was written before Him, for those who feared the Lord and for those who thought upon His Name": And the simple understanding of the verse is about the righteous in the future to come: when people will see their lofty status and say, "For what did this thing come to them," they will answer, "Because earlier 'they spoke one with another' in words of Torah and it was written 'in the book of remembrance' and He is now giving them the reward for their activity".

I have no Scriptural support for this except in a case of two. From where is there proof that that even when there is only one person studying Torah, the Holy One, blessed be He, determines a reward for him: He means to say one who sits and thinks about Torah. Since reward is given for thought as it is for one involved in speech.

As it is said - "He sits alone and is silent, since he takes a reward for it": As one who is silent and thinks about Torah is as if he takes on the yoke of Torah in oral meditation. But

Pirkei Avot - Rabbeinu Yonah - Chapter 3

Rabbi Meir HaLevi follows the textual variant, "From where is there proof that that even when there is only one person studying Torah, the verse equates it for him as if he fulfilled the whole entire Torah, as it is said - "He sits alone and is silent, since he takes a reward for it." And how is it implied that the expression "And he is silent" is about speech? From "Since he takes" which refers to the yoke of speech, as he preaches in front of [the people].

3. Rabbi Shimon said: if three have eaten at one table and have not spoken there words of Torah, it is as if they had eaten sacrifices offered to the dead, as it is said - "for all tables are full of filthy vomit, when the All Present is absent." But, if three have eaten at one table, and have spoken there words of Torah, it is as if they had eaten at the table of the All-Present, blessed be He, as it is said - "And He said unto me, this is the table before the Lord."

Rabbeinu Yonah

Rabbi Shimon says: Three who ate at one table and did not say upon it words of Torah it is as if they ate from the offerings of the dead: He means to say that since they did not say words of Torah, behold all of the tables are as if they were full of offering to idolatry which is considered to be like feces. Since the gathering of three people is called a group, as indicated by the fact that they would have an invitation for the Grace after the meals. And one should not join them if there are no words of Torah among them, as that is removing the yoke of Torah. They are eating and drinking and enjoying, but the mention of Torah does not arise upon their hearts - woe to them and woe to their enjoyment.

However, three who ate at one table and said upon it words of Torah - it is as if they ate from the table of the Omnipresent, blessed be He, as it is said - "And he said to me, this is the table that is before the Lord": And the expression, "And he said," is referring to an individual, as you see with "And the Lord said to Moshe," which is individual, as He was speaking to Moshe alone. And when the verse wants to make the thing communal - for Moshe to say it to Israel - it is written, **saying**; which is a communal language. The explanation of "he said" by itself without "saying" is that He explained it to Moshe only and not that others should hear it. Also, this in which it is stated, "And he said to me, this is the table," is an expression of "and he said" that specifies that this table is from below. Such that you should not think that it specifies that the table is from Above, the sacrificial table of the Temple offerings. And even though this is not a proof for the matter, it is a hint to the matter - as is the custom of our rabbis to use as support in several places.

4. Rabbi Hananiah ben Hakinai said: one who wakes up at night, or walks on the way alone and turns his heart to idle matters, behold, this man is mortally guilty.

<u>Rabbeinu Yonah</u>

Rabbi Chananya ben Chakhinai says, etc. such a one is liable for forfeiture of his life: Since they are desirable times, he should only think during them about things that are desirable before the Omnipresent, may He be blessed. And those things are words of Torah. As how grand and desirable are these times for thinking about Torah, since he has no work to do and does not hear the voices of other people.

And one who turns his heart to idleness, such a one is liable for forfeiture of his life: As he wastes a time in which he can have clear and correct thought, and diverts it from thoughts of Torah.

5. Rabbi Nehunia ben Hakkanah said: whoever takes upon himself the yoke of the Torah, they remove from him the yoke of government and the yoke of worldly concerns, and whoever breaks off from himself the yoke of the Torah, they place upon him the yoke of government and the yoke of worldly concerns.

Rabbeinu Yonah

Rabbi Nechunya ben Hakanah says: Anyone who accepts the yoke of Torah upon himself, they lift from him the yoke of government: The Holy One, blessed be He, guards form every bad thing the one who makes his Torah study primary and his work flexible, so that he not have to refrain from Torah study. And so, He does not put it into the heart of the king - that takes people to do his work - to take this one. And he is saved from the work of the kings to fulfill his will to be involved in Torah.

And the yoke of the way of the world [Derekh erets]: He is not required to do much work for the needs of his livelihood, and he is able to suffice with little for his vital needs, since the work of the righteous is blessed and his soul is glad with his portion.

And anyone who casts from himself the yoke of Torah, they place upon him the yoke of government: Since he thinks that if he leaves the work of Torah, he will do a lot of his work, God, may He be blessed, annuls his thought and puts into the heart of the king to take him to do work for him since - "Like channeled water is the heart of the king in the Lord's hand; He directs it to whatever He wishes".

And the yoke of the way of the world [Aerekh erets]: As he wanders and strains for his livelihood and he cannot find it. Even when he finds it, he is not glad with his portion; and all of his days, he exerts himself in vain to get rich and to add wealth to his wealth. And it is like the matter that is stated - "A lover of money never has his fill of money." And it comes out that all of his days are spent in toil and exertion, and he will never have rest for ever and ever.

6. Rabbi Halafta of Kefar Hanania said: when ten sit together and occupy themselves with Torah, the Shechinah abides among them, as it is said - "God stands in the congregation of God". How do we know that the same is true even of five? As it is said - "This band of His He has established on earth". How do we know that the same is true even of three? As it is said - "In the midst of the judges He judges" How do we know that the same is true even of two? As it is said - "Then they that fear the Lord spoke one with another, and the Lord hearkened, and heard". How do we know that the same is true even of one? As it is said - "In every place where I cause my name to be mentioned I will come unto you and bless you".

Rabbeinu Yonah

Rabbi Chalafta ben Dosa of Kfar [Village] **Chananiah says: Ten who are sitting together and engaging in Torah, the Divine Presence rests among them, as it is said (Psalms 82:1): "God stands in the congregation of God":** And there is no congregation that is less than ten.

And from where is there proof that this is true even when there are only five? As it is said - "And He has founded His band upon the earth:" A hand which has five fingers is called a band [Aguda].

And from where even three? As it is said: "In the midst of judges He judges:" And there is no court that is less than three.

And from where even two? As it is said - "Then those who feared the Lord spoke one with another." And from where even one? As it is said - "In every place where I

cause My Name to be mentioned I will come to you and bless you:" And if even one gets much reward, is it not obvious that from to ten to two, they would also get reward. Rather, he wants to say that to each number, the reward is according to the quantity.

7. Rabbi Elazar of Bartotha said: give to Him of that which is His, for you and that which is yours is His; and thus it says with regards to David - "For everything comes from You, and from Your own hand have we given you." Rabbi Jacob said: if one is studying while walking on the road and interrupts his study and says, "how fine is this tree!" or "how fine is this newly ploughed field!" scripture accounts it to him as if he was mortally guilty.

Rabbeinu Yonah

Rabbi Elazar, man of Bartuta, says: Give Him from what is His: This is speaking whether about the matter of a person's body, whether about the matter of a person's money, and it is to say that a person should not withhold himself nor his money from the objects of Heaven. And this is what he said:

For you and yours are His: As you are not giving from yourself and not from your money, but rather from the Omnipresent, may He blessed, as everything is His. As a person's money is a deposit in his hand from the Holy One, blessed be He, except that there is an advantage with it over other deposits in that he can take from it according to his needs. And he should give the rest in accordance with the will of the Depositor, the King, King of kings, the Holy One, blessed be He who commanded him. And there is much to rejoice in that he can benefit from the deposit in speech the editor says, it appears to me that it should be corrected to, enough for his needs, and that he will do the will of its Owner with the rest. There is a parable relevant to this of a king that gave his servant a thousand zuz and said to him, "Take one hundred for your yourself and give the remaining nine hundred to nine people." Would he not rejoice?

And thus with David it says, "For all comes from You, and from Your hand we have given to You": In another place there it is written - "It is from Your hand, and it is all Yours." And that is stated about the body, that He prepared it to build His holy House. And that which is written, "and from Your hand we have given to You," is stated about the matter of money; as he states at the beginning of the verse, "that we should have the means to make such a freewill offering; for all comes from You, and from Your hand we have given to You."

Rabbi Yaakov says: He who is walking on the way and repeating his studies, and interrupts his studies, etc. As when a person is still studying, he should not be involved in mundane conversation, since he needs to stand in fear and awe in front of the Torah. [It is] like the matter that they said In the Talmud - "Any student who is learning and his lips do not drip with myrrh, let him be burnt." Since he is using the crown of Torah which is the crown of the Holy One, blessed be He, he needs to not speak idly. And if he becomes light-headed to interrupt his studies, behold "he is liable for forfeiture of his life." And this is in line with justice.

8. Rabbi Dostai ben Rabbi Yannai said in the name of Rabbi Meir: whoever forgets one word of his study, scripture accounts it to him as if he were mortally guilty, as it is said, "But take utmost care and watch yourselves scrupulously, so that you do not forget the things that you saw with your own eyes". One could have inferred that this is the case even when his study proved hard for him, therefore scripture says, "that they do not fade from your mind as long as you live". Thus, he is not mortally guilty unless he deliberately removes them from his heart.

Rabbeinu Yonah

Rabbi Dostai beRebbe Yannai in the name of Rabbi Meir says: Anyone who forgets one thing from his studies - Scripture considers him as if he is liable for [forfeiture of] his life, as it is said - "Only guard yourself, etc. As he did not put it into his heart to say that forgetting is common with people. He should have reviewed the law many times and be thinking about it the whole day and the whole night, until it could not leave his heart. And as he did not, he is liable for forfeiture of his life; since he will come to give rulings according to his memory and say, "So said Rabbi." And so he will forbid the permissible and permit the forbidden and a mishap will come from his hand; and he will be called a sinner, for an error in study is considered an intentional transgression.

One could suppose this statement applies to even one whose studies have overpowered him; therefore, the verse says, "and lest they depart from your heart all the days of your life" - he is not liable for forfeiture of his life until he sits down and intentionally removes them from his heart: If he forgot it due to old age, or due to another matter out of his control, the Merciful One exempts him.

9. Rabbi Hanina ben Dosa said: anyone whose fear of sin precedes his wisdom, his wisdom is enduring, but anyone whose wisdom precedes his fear of sin, his wisdom is not enduring. He also used to say: anyone whose deeds exceed his wisdom, his wisdom is enduring, but anyone whose wisdom exceeds his deeds, his wisdom is not enduring.

Rabbeinu Yonah

Rabbi Chanina ben Dosa says: Anyone whose fear of sin precedes his wisdom, his wisdom endures: The matter is said regarding effort - One who makes efforts to know wisdom in order to guard his soul from sin, and he becomes wise; his wisdom endures in his hand. And it comes out that when the studies and becomes enlightened, he removes himself from sins and does a commandment.

And anyone whose wisdom precedes his fear of sin, his wisdom does not endure: He did not make efforts from the beginning to know wisdom in order to observe it, but rather to understand and be enlightened; and so it will not endure in his hand. And this is in line with justice. **Another explanation**: When a person's fear of sin precedes his wisdom, it comes out that when he studied, it guarded him and strengthened him to go on the path that he is accustomed to from many days; since when he fears sin and his heart adds great love for it and desires to add to it, it strengthens him to do that to which he is accustomed. But when the wisdom of a person precedes his fear of sin, it comes out that his wisdom tries to prevent him from sins that he is accustomed to. And in the end, he will rebel against it - as it will appear like a burden to him.

He would also say: Anyone whose actions are more plentiful than his wisdom, his wisdom endures: When a person's actions are more plentiful than his wisdom, it comes out that his desire for wisdom is greater than his wisdom. And it comes out that his he will add wisdom to his wisdom each and every day.

And anyone whose wisdom is more plentiful than his actions, his wisdom does not endure: As it comes out that his desire for wisdom is less than his wisdom, and it will come out that his wisdom will continually lessen. So did the early scholars, may their memory be blessed, explain. However, one should ask, how is it possible for his actions to be greater than his wisdom. If he doesn't know the Torah and the commandments; when he needs to do these actions, upon what basis will he do them? Rather this mishnah was speaking according to a fit, good and accepted advice for the one who doesn't know - so that he not destroys his soul. That advice is that he accept upon himself to do all of the things that the sages tell him to do, and not to veer from them to the right or to the left when he knows them. And he should act according to the Torah that they instruct him and according to the law that they tell him. And immediately when he accepts upon himself this acceptance with a full heart and a desiring soul, he brings himself reward, as if he did all of the commandments. And according to this approach, they said, "Anyone whose actions are more plentiful than his wisdom," as even for the one who does not know and does not do, they are called actions - since he has reward for them as if he did them, on account of his acceptance. And so is it explained in The Fathers According to Rabbi Nathan, as we learned there, "Anyone whose actions are more plentiful than his wisdom, his wisdom endures, as it is stated, we shall do and we shall understand." As Israel had doing precede understanding, whereas they should have said, "we will understand and we will do" - as before one can do an action, they need to understand what to do. However, they accepted upon themselves first to do all that He would command them and that they would understand; and they received reward from it immediately as if they had done them. "And anyone whose wisdom is more plentiful than his actions, etc." - that he should not say, "I will study this law and then I will practice it, I will study the whole Talmud and then I will practice it." If he says like this, his wisdom will not endure - as one needs to perfect the traits first and then his wisdom will endure.

10. He used to say: one with whom men are pleased, God is pleased. But anyone from whom men are displeased, God is displeased. Rabbi Dosa ben Harkinas said: morning sleep, midday wine, children's talk and sitting in the assemblies of the ignorant put a man out of the world.

Rabbeinu Yonah

He would say: Anyone from whom the spirit of creations find pleasure, from him the spirit of God finds pleasure: He wanted to say, one whose give and take business dealings is pleasant for people and they all know that he is considered trustworthy by the creatures. And it is like we say in Talmud - "Any scholar who reads and studies and gives and takes with trustworthiness among the creatures, what do the creatures say about him? Happy is his father, happy is his mother happy is his rabbi that taught him Torah, etc." And because of this, "from him the spirit of God finds pleasure," since the Torah is lauded through him.

And anyone from whom the spirit of creations do not find pleasure, from him the spirit of God does not find pleasure: He will not 'be innocent from God and from Israel.

Rabbi Dosa ben Harkinus says: Late morning sleep: As it negates prayer at its time.

midday wine: As it negates Torah study and so leads to sin.

chatter of children: As this playing draw in the hearts of people because of their love for youngsters, and it comes out that Torah study is neglected.

And sitting in the assembly houses of the Am Ha'arets [unlearned people, who are lax in observing tithes and purity laws]: And many evils are found in their assembly houses.

Pirkei Avot - Rabbeinu Yonah - Chapter 3

Remove a person from the world: Since for what was man created besides to be involved with Torah, and it is 'the length of days and the years of life? And if he engages in such things, why does he have life? And it is fit to drive him from the world, as he is vanity and his days are vanity. And since he has lived some years and has been involved in his affairs and it has not helped, because he has neglected Torah, for what reason should his days be increased? There is parable relevant to this about a king that gave his servant one hundred silver coins, and he threw them into the sea, and then returned and requested others from him. And is it not fit that he not give him more? So is it with one who does not involve himself with Torah.

11. Rabbi Elazar of Modiin said: one who profanes sacred things, and one who despises the festivals, and one who causes his fellow's face to blush in public, and one who annuls the covenant of our father Abraham, may he rest in peace, and he who is contemptuous towards the Torah, even though he has to his credit [knowledge of the] Torah and good deeds, he has not a share in the world to come.

Rabbeinu Yonah

Rabbi Elazar of Modi'in says: One who profanes the Kodeshim [Sacred material]: This is one who intends to delay their consumption and so renders them impure. It is the same whether it is sacred material for the altar or whether it is sacred material for the upkeep of the House [Bedek Habayit] if he profanes them, he has no share in the world to come.

One who desecrates the holidays: He made these two things adjacent because they are both called holy things. With holy material, it is written - "holy of holies"; and with holidays, it is written - these are "the holidays of the Lord, which you shall proclaim, holy proclamations." And about this the rabbis, may their memory be blessed, said - "Anyone who profanes the holidays - it is as if he worships idolatry, as it is stated - You shall not make molten gods for yourselves. And it placed it adjacent to. You shall observe the Feast of Unleavened Bread." And he said here, "one who desecrates" and he did not say, "one who profanes the holidays," because he is not speaking about the festival day itself - as about this it is not required to speak, since a festival day is like Shabbat. Rather, he is speaking about the intermediate days of the holiday [Chol hamoed]; about the one doing forbidden work with his hand. And such a one may say, "These days do not have so much holiness, like the first festival days." And so, he does every work and disgusting thing on them, yet he will not feel shame.

One who nullifies the covenant of Abraham our father: This is one who pulls his foreskin to cover his corona and he appears like an uncircumcised one - it is like one who does it to anger, to disgrace the commandments.

one who whitens [Embarrasses] **the face of another in public**: This is a derivative of the things for which he should die and not transgress. And the sources avot of the derivatives are three: idolatry, forbidden sexual relations and the spilling of blood murder. The derivative of idolatry is the wood that comes from a tree-god [Ashera]; and like we say - "We may heal ourselves with anything, except for the wood of a tree-god." And even though it is not necessarily idolatry itself; but rather even when it is its auxiliary, he should die and not transgress rather than benefiting from it. And the derivative of sexual relations is one who stares at or converses with a married woman - that he should die and not transgress. It is like that case in - about the one whose heart became sick with lust about whom they said, "That she stands before him naked - He should rather die; she will not stand before him naked! That she should speak with him from behind a fence - he should rather die; she will not speak with him from behind a fence." And the derivative of spilling blood is "one who whitens the face of another in public" - since his blood flees from the embarrassment. It is as we say - "We see that the red leaves and white comes in its place." And because of this, he has no share in the world to come.

One who reveals meanings in the Torah that run contrary to the law: This is one who makes his face brazen towards the Torah, to do sins in public. And the same is true of one who makes his face brazen towards its learners.

even though he has Torah knowledge and good deeds, he has no share in the world to come: And these words relate to when he has not repented, but rather died with afflictions

- as death and afflictions do not atone in this case. But if he has repented, there is nothing for you that stands in front of that is resistant to repentance. And so is it learned in the gemara.

12. Rabbi Ishmael said: be suppliant to a superior, submissive under compulsory service, and receive every man happily.

Rabbeinu Yonah

Rabbi Yishmael says: Be yielding to an elder literally a head: He wants to say, that he be yielding to one who is a head and a lord, as it is stated - "Do not exalt yourself in the king's presence; do not stand in the place of great ones" - that you should not think of yourself as a great man, but lower yourself in front of him to do his desires and to fulfill his needs. And do not become too familiar with him.

Pleasant to a tishchoret: Meaning to say to be pleasant with his words to an appointed official. Not that he lowers himself in front of him, as he is not a lord; and not that he should try to overcome him, as the official also has power in his hand: since he judges the land and the king appointed him over his people, it is impossible that he will not think about doing bad to his enemies; and he can truly do it to them. But one can benefit from his friendship, as he is like the master of the land. And tishchoret is the same as shichvar. In the vernacular, it is señorío. And [it is] as we say - "Cling to the shichvar and they will bow down to you." and greet every person with joy. And Rabbi Meir HaLevi, may his memory be blessed, explains tishchoret from the translation of "I have not taken the donkey of any one of them" as shecharit. He wants to say that you should be pleasant with a great person and a head, and also be pleasant with his servant and do his will.

13. Rabbi Akiva said: Merriment and frivolity accustom one to sexual licentiousness; Tradition is a fence to the Torah; Tithes a fence to wealth, Vows a fence to abstinence; A fence to wisdom is silence.

Rabbeinu Yonah

Rabbi Akiva says: Joking and lightheartedness acclimate toward promiscuity: He wants to say that joking and words of idle conversation with lightheartedness acclimates to promiscuity. But seriousness and fear are a safeguarding fence around sexual prohibitions - as this whole mishnah is talking about safeguarding fences.

Tithes are a safeguarding fence around wealth: And like we say - About that child that was reading "A tithe shall you tithe [**Aaser teaser**]" - Rabbi Yochanan said to him, "Take a tithe so that you will become wealthy." The boy said to him, "And is it permitted to test the Holy One, Blessed be He? But it is written - You shall not test the Lord your God?" Rabbi Yochanan said to him, "Rabbi Hoshaya said as follows, Except for this, as it is stated - "Bring the whole tithe into the storeroom, that there may be food in My house, and test Me now by this". And about this is it said, "Tithes are a safeguarding fence around wealth" - that the person that wants to be wealthy should give tithes with a good eye. And he should not say, "I have a thousand kor [About 250 liters] - how can I give a hundred to the tithe, and they are worth much." As God, may He be blessed and elevated, is trustworthy to pay him all that he gave and to multiply the reward. And this is true also based on experience. And the matter of charity is like the matter of tithes - and so when he increases charity, he adds wealth to his wealth. And a person's heart should not prevent him from giving large gifts to the needy, lest his wealth shrink and he not have enough. And he will know that this will be the reason that he will have a right to make wealth. And the very wealthy one should not think that by his giving much charity - if he doesn't give proportionately according to his wealth and multitude of assets - that he will be innocent. As an evil thing may come into his heart to say, "How many coins have I scattered in charity; how many, many were dying of hunger and I saved them." And he does not know about all this, that the poor person who gives a 'great sum' according to the tithe is better off. As in the case of a poor man who only has a seah and gives its tithe as is fit and a wealthy man who has two thousand seah and gives one less than two hundred; the poor man gets out innocent, but the rich man is still obligated by them. So is it with charity: everyone must give according to what he has - whether it is little or whether it is much.

Tradition is a safeguarding fence around Torah: Traditions are the full spellings and incomplete spellings of the words in the Torah and the cantillation notes that the sages passed on to their students. And they are a safeguarding fence around the written Torah, such that you do not find differences among the books [of the Torah], except in a few places. This is not the case with the books of the Talmud, as in many places the versions differ. Also, each and every day, new rationales are developed - and they write the version according to their opinion. And the right has been given to tolerate it. As there is no perfect book in the world that they have not made to err. And they attribute the mistake to the book and not to their opinion.

Vows are a safeguarding fence around abstinence: Abstinence is a superior virtue and there are several good virtues that are needed to acquire it, as we say - "Cleanliness leads to abstinence." And this is one who separates from the pleasures of the world - even from the things that are permissible in eating and sexual relations; even from all of the other desires in avoiding honor and lordship and wealth and what is similar to them. And he distances himself from the roots of the pleasures and brings himself near to the fundamentals [Literally, Trunks] of the soul and its foundation. And hence he is close to the service of the

Creator, may He be blessed. How is it with food? One who eats a little in order to live that he be healthy to study much Torah and to do great service in the service of God. And he drinks to fill his thirst and not to get drunk and so not expose himself within his tent. And that which he only has sexual relations to fulfill the commandment, behold this is from the way of abstinence - as his intention is not to enjoy from the world. And there is also a second benefit: that he guard his soul from sin, as when his impulse overpowers him and he desires to do a sin, he will say in his heart, "I am vigilant about what is permissible, so how can I do this great evil, and I will have sinned to my Father in heaven all of the days." And this thing will protect him from all of the stumbling blocks. But one who goes after natural physicality and is pulled by his desires and his pleasures - even if he does not do a forbidden thing - will be found to have distanced himself from the fundamentals of his soul and its foundation. He will have also caused his soul to follow the body and the physical and 'sever it with an ax from its roots and its foundation.' And [it is] as it is written - "Promiscuity, wine and new wine take the heart." Hence, they gave a counsel to the one who is not able to lead to control his spirit and is pulled by the pleasures, to make a vow for some days to say, "I will not eat and not drink until specific time except like this"; or to forbid what is permissible. And then his habit will control him, from that which he observes his vow. It comes out that he leads himself to conquer his impulse. And with this, the benefit that is in his hand is abstinence. And it is as someone said to Rabbi Pinchas "If you are not able to eat mundane foods in purity all of the year, eat it so for seven days." As one who eats mundane foods in purity is called an abstinent, as we say - "The clothes of an ignoramus are impure in midras for the abstinent prushim." However, it is not fit to fence oneself with fences unless his impulse is overpowering him, and then] he may make a vow as a way of healing. However, one who controls his spirit and is able to reach the trait of abstinence without a vow should not vow. It is as we said - "Is it not enough for you with what the Torah forbade, such that you forbid yourself the permitted?" But certainly, if you see a man whose impulse is overpowering him, he needs to add a big fence according to that which he needs to conquer his impulse. And once he has conquered his impulse, he goes back to the moderate disposition. There is a parable about a physician relevant to this: When the physician sees that the illness is mild and easy to heal, he gives him a mild treatment. But when he sees that he illness is heavy and strong, he chooses a strong treatment until he heals; and afterwards, he goes back and gives him moderate things that hold the body's health. And because of this, they said, "Vows are a safeguarding fence around abstinence" - and they did not say, "Oaths are a safeguarding fence around abstinence." As an oath halts immediately, as he swears that he will not eat this thing until specific day. And that is not a safeguarding fence - as he is halted immediately, in that he cannot transgress it. But a vow is that he says, "If I eat more than this amount until specific day, all of the fruits of the world will be forbidden until a different time that he specifies. That is called a safeguarding fence, as it is a thing that he may overstep. And it is better for the one whose heart is dedicated to the Heavens if he is not in control of himself to do the safeguarding fence without a vow.

A safeguarding fence around wisdom is silence: This is a safeguarding fence for both wisdom itself and for its traits. How is it? That he doesn't interrupt the words of his fellow, and he says about that we has not heard, "I have not heard." And even though it is not included in silence, silence brings to it. With wisdom, how is it? He does not speak in front of someone greater than him in wisdom. As one who studies in front of his teacher and sees a fit rationale should not immediately think that it is true; and he should not want to say it until his teacher has finished speaking. For were he to do so, he would miss what his teacher will say and he will not know the rationales of the earlier sages; as his heart will be moving and wandering from knowing their opinion. And also, because his own rationale cannot be so focused until he hears what the early scholars said and then weigh in the scales of his intellect which one is more proper - this one or that one. Therefore, silence for a student in front of his teacher "is a safeguarding fence for wisdom." And when he finds a rationale and his teacher is still speaking, should he not be quiet? He should not open his mouth until the words of his teacher are clear and his rationale is etched into his heart - until he finishes his words and knows what his teacher taught him. And afterwards, his reasoning will be sharp and focused. And about this Shlomo, peace be upon him, said - "The fool does not desire understanding, but only to reveal his heart".

14. He used to say: Beloved is man for he was created in the image of God. Especially beloved is he for it was made known to him that he had been created in the image of God, as it is said - "for in the image of God He made man". Beloved are Israel in that they were called children to the All-Present. Especially beloved are they for it was made known to them that they are called children of the All-Present, as it is said - "Your are children to the Lord your God". Beloved are Israel in that a precious vessel was given to them. Especially beloved are they for it was made known to them that the desirable instrument, with which the world had been created, was given to them, as it is said - "for I give you good instruction; forsake not my teaching".

Rabbeinu Yonah

He would say: Beloved is man, since he is created in the image of God. A deeper love - it is revealed to him that he is created in the image, as it says - "for in God's image He made man": Since he doubled the expression, we should say that this is its explanation: "Beloved is man since he is created in the image" - as even if the thing was not made known, but man was still created in the image of God, he would be beloved in front of Him; since they were created in His image and in His likeness. But when He revealed the thing to us, He showed us a deeper love.

Beloved are Israel, since they are called children of the Omnipresent. A deeper love - it is revealed to them that they are called children to God, as it says - "You are children of the Lord, your God": Also, since he doubled it like the first.

Beloved are Israel, since a precious instrument has been

Pirkei Avot - Rabbeinu Yonah - Chapter 3

given to them: With which the world was created - this is the Torah, since the whole world was created with it; and all of the creatures were only created so as to observe it. And everything under the skies - all of them - are a function of a function for the needs of the practitioners of the Torah. There is a metaphor relevant to this about one who makes a tool for his profession and, with it, he does all of his work. So too is the Torah the tool of the Holy One, blessed be He, and with it the whole entire world was created.

A deeper love it is revealed to them that the precious instrument with which the world was created has been given to them: With which the world was created.

As it says - "For a good lesson I have given to you; do not forsake my teaching": And you should know that these words are of great benefit for devotion to God - since he revealed to us that man is more beloved in front of Him than all of the creatures because he is created in the image; and that Israel know that they are more beloved than all of the other peoples since they are called the children of the Omnipresent and He chose us from all of the nations and gave us His Torah, as a function of which the whole entire world was created. So, by all events, we know that God, may He be blessed and exalted, is close to us. Still a person should not think that if he does what is 'straight in the eyes of the Lord' and not sin that he is close to God, as you know that the grasp of man is limited and not complete such that he can reach devotion to God. And yet it should not appear to him that He is completely far from him - "a deeper love is revealed to" him if he is from the seed of the Jews. And he should not be in his own eyes only an evildoer and not only righteous. And this is the teaching of man - not to distance himself and not to come close, and all is in accordance to the majority of the deed. As with the great devotion involved here, how can we have it - and there is no man on the earth that does good and does not sin. It is as Yirmiyahu said - "His chieftain shall be one of his own, his ruler shall come from his midst; I will bring him near that he may approach Me, declares the Lord; for who is it who would pledge yeaarev his heart to approach Me?" And aarev here is an expression of aarevut [Guarantee].

15. Everything is foreseen yet freedom of choice is granted, And the world is judged with goodness; And everything is in accordance with the preponderance of works.

Rabbeinu Yonah

Everything is foreseen: As it is written - "Lord, You have examined me and know. When I sit down or stand up You know it; You discern my thoughts from afar, etc".

And freewill is given: As He gave into the hand of people to do all that his heart desires - whether good or whether bad; as it is stated - "See, I set before you, etc." And Rambam, may his memory be blessed, said that this thing is from the wonders: That even though freewill is given to man to do his will, the Holy One, blessed be He, knows what he will want to do before the thought and before the action. And not by force will a man do the good or the bad, but rather from the will of his own heart. And God, may He be blessed, knows at the beginning that which will be his will - and even those things that are weighed out and it is possible that they will be and possible that they will not be. He knows everything at the beginning of the deed, and it is a wonder.

And with goodness the world is judged: And the Holy One, blessed be He, does not judge man only according to his deeds - rather also with His Goodness and His trait of kindness. And this is what David said - "Be not mindful of my youthful sins and my transgressions." Sins - whether they are accidental or volitional - are what a man does in his youth, when his impulse impels him and his intellect is weak. However, those that he does after he has grown in years and his intellect is complete are called transgressions or rebellion. And because of this, he confessed and said, "Both the sins of my youth and the transgressions from after I grew up, do not remember; and so too let my memory go up in front of You, remember me for the good. But in keeping with Your kindness, You remember me - as befits Your goodness, Lord." As the world is judged with kindness, and even evildoers are judged with His goodness, as it is stated - "Good is the Lord to all and His mercies are to all of His creatures." And the evildoers are included in His creatures - of the Holy One, blessed be He - as it is found in the midrash.

And all is in accordance to the majority of the deed: And even though the world is judged with the good of the Lord, not every person is equal with God's trait of good. As for one who does much kindliness, the trait of kindness is much more than his deeds, and for the one who does little, it is little more. And if all are judged with His goodness, yet the good beyond the deeds of the evildoers is not as much as for the righteous; and also, the righteous who do much and those who do a little are not the same, as "all is in accordance to the majority of the deed." And it is like it is said in the midrash - "The Lord is good to those who hope in Him", to the soul that seeks Him - the one who hopes and is busy with it is not similar to the one who hopes and is not busy." And our teacher Moshe the **Rambam**, may his memory be blessed, followed the textual variant, "but not according to the deed. And he explained that all is according to the majority quantity of the deed. As in the matter of charity, one who gives a thousand zuz over a thousand times, that is according to the quantity of the deed; but "not according to the deed" - that is the one gives it all at once. As this one arouses his thought a thousand times to do good among his people, and that one only aroused it the first time.

16. He used to say: everything is given against a pledge, and a net is spread out over all the living; the store is open and the storekeeper allows credit, but the ledger is open and the hand writes, and whoever wishes to borrow may come and borrow; but the collectors go round regularly every day and exact dues from man, either with his consent or without his consent, and they have that on which they can rely in their claims, seeing that the judgment is a righteous judgment, and everything is prepared for the banquet.

Rabbeinu Yonah

He would say: Everything is given as collateral: For everything that a person takes from this world, he is a guarantor and his children are guarantors. And one who inherits his father and his mother should not think, "This money is my inheritance, I will do all that I want with it." As nothing that he has is his, since everything is God's. And that which he took from Him, he took it on collateral; and in the future he will have to pay for it. There is a parable [relevant to this] about a man that came into a city and did not find anybody there. He went into a house and there he found a set table and all types of food and drink were upon it. He ate and drank and said, "Have I not acquired all of this, and it is all mine - I will do all that I want with it." And he did not see the owners who were observing him from another place. And in the future, he will have to pay for all that he will eat and drink, as he is in a place that he cannot escape.

And a net is cast over all of life: This is death and a person cannot be saved from it - like fish caught in a bad net.

The shop is open: As people go in there and take all that they need now and don't see what will come from it. And they don't think if they will have with what to pay when it comes time for the payment, since they find the store open and they can take all of their needs at the time. Such are people in this world.

And the shopkeeper grants credit: This is the owner of the store who gives to others on credit - he is the judge and is paid by them later. So is the Ruler over His world: He gives all the wants of those that come to the world - whether good or whether bad - and in the end, He will be payed by them later.

And the accounting ledger is open: This thing is said for two matters. The one is a metaphor that there is no forgetting in front of His throne of glory. As the shopkeeper grants credit, he grants credit and lends to many people - to some for thousands and tens of thousand, and to some for one dinar, And for an error, Were it not for his alacrity that the ledger is open in front of him and he immediately writes everything, sometimes he would forget the small things because of the big ones - if he would lend orally. And about this is it said, "and the accounting ledger is open, and the hand writes." This is to say with both the big sins and the small ones - all of them - it is as if they are written in front of Him; and he does not forget the earlier transgressions. And the second matter is to inform us that there is no waiting for the opening of the ledger after he does the sin. Rather with the end of the act, it is already written; so that an instant not pass that this transgression is not attributed to him. As even though transgressions are forgiven to penitents, they are first attributed immediately when they are finished doing them. And afterwards if he repents, he is forgiven for them. It is as we say in the midrash, "One who does not do it, is not like the one who does it and is forgiven" - as the one who does not do is greater than the one that does and is forgiven. And regarding that which it said - "The completely righteous cannot stand in the place that the penitents stand," it wanted to say that penitents have to separate from that which is permissible but similar to the matter in which they sinned. As if he transgressed sexual prohibitions, he should act with abstinence towards the thing that he sinned in - even with his wife and even with what is permissible - more than the completely righteous need to do.

And everyone who wants to borrow can come and borrow: As permission to do so is given to every man, and the one that wants to take the path that he desires, let him come and take: The fools thinks that the world was created to enjoy it, but all of the thoughts and the pleasure of the righteous is to be free to fulfill the commandments. And every man chooses for himself, but happy is the one who chooses the good.

And the collectors go constantly on their daily rounds: from the Heavens. As they search through the actions of people, as it is stated - "You inspect him in the mornings" to know and make known what they are doing.

And exact payment from man with his knowledge: How is it? When he knows and remembers the sin that he does; so, that when the punishment come to him, he recognizes and discerns that it is for that sin. And happy is he, as through this, he justifies the judgement and repents; and the sin is atoned for him.

Or without his knowledge: How is it? For example, when afflictions come to him and he does not remember the sins that he did. And there are some that think that the afflictions come to them unjustly, as they say, "We are righteous and we have not sinned, and why is there this great evil that has come to us." And they will die without repentance. And their worms will not die, as they vilified the judgement and justified themselves. Woe to them and woe to their carcasses - as they sinned against their bodies. There is a parable relevant to this about a king that said to his servant, "Go and take collateral from one." So, he went and took collateral from him, but that man does not remember the debt. And he yells and is in wonder about why they are taking collateral from him, and it is given over to his heart he is distressed about it. Such is the one who payment is taken from, from the Heavens, without his knowledge. But when he remembers the debt and knows that the taking of collateral is justified, the matter is not given over to his heart so much.

And they have that upon which to rely: for their deeds: Upon God's trait of justice, and the judgement is true judgement.

And everything is prepared for the feast: That the purpose of all of these things is in the end only to prepare the feast; meaning to say for life in the world to come.

17. Rabbi Elazar ben Azariah said: Where there is no Torah, there is no right conduct; where there is no right conduct, there is no Torah. Where there is no wisdom there is no fear of God; where there is no fear of God, there is no wisdom. Where there is no understanding, there is no knowledge; where there is no knowledge, there is no understanding. Where there is no bread, there is no Torah; where there is no Torah, there is no bread. He used to say: one whose wisdom exceeds his deeds, to what may he be compared? To a tree whose branches are numerous but whose roots are few, so that when the wind comes, it uproots it and overturns it, as it is said, "He shall be like a bush in the desert, which does not sense the coming of good. It is set in the scorched places of the wilderness, in a barren land without inhabitant". But one whose deeds exceed his wisdom, to what may he be compared? To a tree whose branches are few but roots are many, so that even if all the winds in the world come and blow upon it, they cannot move it out of its place, as it is said, "He shall be like a tree planted by waters, sending forth its roots by a stream. It does not sense the coming of heat, its leaves are ever fresh. It has no care in a year of drought; it does not cease to yield fruit".

<u>Rabbeinu Yonah</u>

Rabbi Elazar ben Azariah says: If there is no Torah, there is no worldly occupation Derekh Erets; literally, the way of the world]: Meaning to say that one who does not know Torah is not complete in the traits of **Derekh Erets**; as most of the good traits that exist in the ways of the world are in the

Torah - like "surely lend him" - "Surely award him" - "Just scales, just weights" - and many, many like these. If so, without Torah, his dispositions in Derekh Erets will not be complete.

If there is no worldly occupation, there is no Torah: He wants to say that he first has to perfect himself in his traits. And through this, the Torah will rest upon him, as it never rests upon a body that is not in possession of good traits. And he should not learn Torah and afterwards take the commandments for himself, as this is impossible. And this is like the matter that is stated - "we will do and we will understand," and like we have written about it.

If there is no wisdom, there is no fear: As there can be no complete fear without wisdom, as it holds it and gives light to lead him on the proper path.

If there is no fear, there is no wisdom: As he needs to have fear precede wisdom. As without this, the wisdom will not last in the end - as he will be sick of it and leave it. Since if he does not first have perfection of the traits and he does not fear God, what good is the cost in the hand of a fool to purchase wisdom, when he has no heart to fulfill the word of God. As fear needs to come before wisdom.

If there is no knowledge, there is no understanding: There are three brains and they are divided to contain three things - wisdom, understanding and knowledge. **Wisdom** is that which he learns from others. **Understanding** is that which he derives one thing from another by comparison. **Knowledge** is that which he grasps on his own. And that which they said, "If there is no knowledge, there is no understanding," is because if he does not have the ability to grasp and know a thing itself on his own, how will he derive something by comparison to something else? As knowledge precedes understanding; and without knowledge, it is impossible that he have understanding.

If there is no understanding, there is no knowledge: If he does not have the power to understand things by comparison to another thing, it is because he does not have complete knowledge to grasp and understand that thing from which he seeks to understand, itself.

If there is no flour, there is no Torah: Because he will need to search for his livelihood and he will not be able to be involved in Torah study.

If there is no Torah, there is no flour: Meaning to say, since he has no Torah, no purpose comes from the flour. As a man only gains from his wealth that the needs of his body be found and that he be free to be involved in Torah.

He would say: Anyone whose wisdom exceeds his deeds, to what is he compared? To a tree whose branches are many but whose roots are few; and the wind comes and uproots it and turns it upside down, etc. But one whose deeds exceed his wisdom, what is he like? Like a tree whose branches are few but whose roots are many; since even if all the winds of the world come and blow upon it, they do not move it from its place: And we have already explained these things in this chapter regarding "Anyone whose fear of sin precedes his wisdom, his wisdom endures, etc."

18. Rabbi Eliezer Hisma said: the laws of mixed bird offerings and the key to the calculations of menstruation days these, these are the body of the halakhah. The calculation of the equinoxes and gematria are the desserts of wisdom.

Rabbeinu Yonah

Rabbi Eliezer ben Chisma says: The laws of Kinin [Bird Offerings]: The offering of doves by women who give birth.

And the beginnings of Niddah [menstruation]: They are three anatomical places - the **house**, the **attic**, and the **entrance hall**; and also, the many sightings of blood that exist with menstruant bloods, these are the body of the laws. And it is like they said - "They brought sixty sightings of blood in front of him, and he determined all of them to be pure [non-menstrual] blood".

Astronomical calculations and Gematria [numerical calculations]: As they contain many calculations, and the wisdom of mathematics sharpens a man.

Are the condiments to wisdom:

Chapter 4

1. Ben Zoma said: Who is wise? He who learns from every man, as it is said - "From all who taught me have I gained understanding". Who is mighty? He who subdues his evil inclination, as it is said - "He that is slow to anger is better than the mighty; and he that rules his spirit than he that takes a city". Who is rich? He who rejoices in his lot, as it is said - "You shall enjoy the fruit of your labors, you shall be happy and you shall prosper." You shall be happy in this world, "and you shall prosper" in the world to come. Who is he that is honored? He who honors his fellow human beings as it is said - "For I honor those that honor Me, but those who spurn Me shall be dishonored."

<u>Rabbeinu Yonah</u>

Ben Zoma said, "Who is the wise one? He who learns from all men: The sages of the nations of the world have said one who knows all of the wisdoms yet does not love wisdom is not a wise man but a fool. As he does not love knowledge, which is intelligence. However, one who loves and desires it - even though he does not know anything - behold, this one is called a wise man. In any event, he will reach true wisdom and find knowledge of God. And about this Ben Zoma said, "Who is the wise one? He who learns from all men" - as so much does he love wisdom that he asks it from every person. And even from the one who only knows one thing does he learn; and then his path becomes successful and he will become enlightened. And because of this he is called a wise one, as it says - "I have acquired understanding from all my teachers". As so did David, peace be upon him, say - that he learned from every person; and he did not say, "This one is not as knowledgeable as I." Rather he learned from them all and became enlightened. There is a metaphor relevant to this about a man that lost a small vessel - would he not seek it from every man?

Who is the mighty one? He who conquers his impulse: Just as the power of the body is its virtue and its distinction, so too is the power of the soul is its virtue. And regarding the power of the body in man, it is also in animals - as they all have the power to lift weights and some more than others - such that Ben Zoma did not speak about it, as it is not called might. Rather he spoke about the might of the heart - which has two powers, to be mighty in war and that his heart never be afraid; and also, the power to subdue the impulse. And this is dissimilar for man and beast, as animals do not have might of the heart. And about this, Ben Zoma said that the braver and stronger power of the heart is that which overcomes the impulse. As might in war is not such a great thing and like you, like them, in the description of men - if they have power, this one also has strength, if they prepared their hands for battle, their fingers for war. But to overcome the impulse - the enemy of a person in his face - and to destroy him, that is an elevated and strong might.

As it says - "slowness to anger is better than a mighty person and the ruler of his spirit than the conqueror of a city.": Slowness to anger describes the one who holds his anger and his will is not to take revenge immediately, but to wait for the time and place of his vengeance. As the angry one that takes revenge immediately, confounds his actions and acts without intelligence. And about this, Shlomo, peace be upon him, stated, "slowness to anger is better than a mighty person." The one who holds his anger - even though he does not forgive during his anger - since he leaves the matter of revenge until later, shows more might of the heart than the mighty one in war; as also without intelligence can he be mighty in fighting. But "the ruler of his spirit" - which is more than one who is slow of anger, since he forgives during his anger, as he fears the word of God - is mightier "than the conqueror of a city." This is even though the latter has two things - might of the heart and wisdom, as it is stated - "A wise man climbed to a city of warriors, and brought down its mighty stronghold." As it is with might of the heart, wisdom and correct counsel that they conquer cities. And about this it is stated - "counsel and might for war." And the ruler of his spirit is greater and more significant than all of this and he comes out overcoming his impulse from all bad things.

Who is the rich one? He who is happy with his lot: This is the one who says, "I have enough with my lot: since I am able to support myself and my household and to engage in Torah study, what is there for me with any other money - it is only for me to have what I need and to uphold the word of God." As one who is not happy with his lot and is not satisfied with what God, may He be blessed, gave him is a poor person; as it is explained in the verse - "All the days of a poor man are bad, but one with a good heart has a constant feast." He wanted to say in this verse that all the days of a 'poor man' that desires money are bad - a lover of money never has his fill of money: but all the days of the one with a good heart, who is happy with his lot, are good as the one like one who makes a constant feast. Hence it is an extremely good trait to be happy with his lot. And he is called rich, since God, may He be blessed, gave him with what to support himself and engage in Torah and in the commandments. As what is the advantage to man in all of his toil, except to fulfill the Torah and the commandments.

As it says, "When you eat from the work of your hands, you will be happy, and it will be well with you". "You will be happy" in this world, and "it will be well with you" in the world to come: This verse is not a proof about the matter that one who is happy with his lot is called rich. Rather, it shows that a person is happy also with this good trait: when he does not desire to gather money and he hates gifts. Instead, he eats from the work of his hands and suffices with it, like the one who is happy with his lot - as his want is only to support himself. And Ben Zoma arranged these three traits like the order of Yirmiyahu the prophet, peace be upon him: wisdom, might and wealth, as it is stated - "Let not the wise man glory in his wisdom; let not the mighty man glory in his might; let not the rich man glory in his wealth." He had wisdom precede might because it is a true virtue and it is in the intellect of the soul and sits in the body, not like might which is only in the body. Still, might is more elevated than wealth, since might is in his body - something that exists all the days that he is still alive - whereas wealth is outside of his body. And it is something transient, as he can make his wealth, and others take it after only half of his days. And even though the prophet stated that a man should not glory in these three traits, Ben Zoma made a distinction and said that there is a side of these traits that is without [physical] exertion and toil and that he can glory in: With wisdom, it is to be one learning from every man. As such, he will understand fear of God; and there is no exertion in it, as it is wisdom and not work. With might, it is to overcome his impulse and to forgive during his anger. In this too he can glory, since he is doing it from his fear of God. And this is what Shlomo, peace be upon him, stated - "It is the intellect of a man that is slow to anger; it is his glory when he overlooks an offense." And since the desire of the one who is happy with his lot is only to learn and to keep the commandments, and when he has enough for his livelihood and support, he is happy and recognizes that the rest is vanity, he is the 'rich' man who can glory in his wealth. As in all of these things, there is knowledge of the Creator, may He be blessed. It is as it is stated - "But only in this should the one who glories glory, in his using his intellect and knowing Me; that I the Lord act with kindness, justice, and equity in the world; for in these I delight, declares the Lord." And Ben Zoma added a fourth trait and said:

Who is honored? He who honors the created beings: One who honors his fellow, honors himself - not his fellow. As what benefit is there to a man if they give him honor? If he is honored, the honor that they gave to him does not add to his status and his honor. And if he is lowly, for others to honor him will not make him honored again. And all honor for the lowly is a loss for those that honor him, as his status is not increased. It is like Shlomo, peace be upon him, stated - "Like binding a stone in a sling, so is paying honor to a fool." As one who binds a stone in a sling is doing nonsense; and there is no honor given to the rock - as it was not elevated by this. And so too is it nonsense to give honor to a fool. It comes out that you will say that with all the honor that a person does to the created beings, he is honoring himself. This is because he causes them perforce to honor him and it will be considered a debt, which is true honor. And about this is it said, "Who is honored? He who honors the created beings".

As it says - "For those who honor Me, I will honor; and those who despise Me will be held in little esteem": And the proof of this verse is from an a fortiori argument [kal vechomer]: If with the Holy One, blessed be He, that all of His creatures were only created for His glory, as it is stated - "that I have created for My honor", and it would not be justified to owe them good for this, since they were not created for anything else and this is their work, and they have no right to do anything else nonetheless, it stated, "For those who honor Me, I will honor"; all the more so and all the more so with regard to his fellows who a person is not obligated to honor, that if he honors him, he will honor him back, and raise him on his palms. And also, with this trait there is no toil, and it is fitting and accepted.

2. Ben Azzai said: Be quick in performing a minor commandment as in the case of a major one, and flee from transgression; For one commandment leads to another commandment, and transgression leads to another transgression; For the reward for performing a commandment is another commandment and the reward for committing a transgression is a transgression.

Rabbeinu Yonah

Ben Azai says: Run to do an easy commandment: They already said a reason for this thing - "for you do not know the reward given for the fulfillment of the respective commandments". And now Ben Azai added another reason and said - **Run to do an easy commandment and flee from sin; since a commandment leads to another commandment**, as this is a natural propensity. As when a man does a small commandment once, he draws closer to God and accustoms his spirit to His service and it becomes easier in his eyes to do another commandment that requires the same effort as the first one or a little more; as he is already accustomed to the performance of a commandment. And when he does a second and a third, even if it is much more effort than the first ones, he will do it quickly, since the habit already steers him greatly. This occurs until it steers him very much and he will completely do all of the commandments.

And a sin leads to another sin: This too is natural. Since he has done one sin and distanced himself from the service of God, may He be blessed, when another sin comes to his hand even if the impulse does not have a desire for it like for the first, he will do it; as his spirit is accessible to his impulse and it pushes upon it. And even if his desire is not great in the matter, he will do all of the sins; as his nature is used to doing every abomination towards God that He hates.

Since the reward for a commandment is another commandment: This is a reason other than nature, And so he wants to say that the Holy One, blessed be He, did not give good or evil into the hand of a person; rather only choice, as it is stated - "and you shall choose life." And since he has chosen a path, if he is going in the good, God is with him. And so, if he does one commandment, it helps him to do another commandment as on his own, he doesn't even have the ability to do good. And about this it says - **since the reward for a commandment is another commandment, and the reward for a sin is another sin**. And not, God forbid, that this is his reward. As if so, what reward does he actually have? And the thing is not like this, as his reward exists for the world to come. But rather he wants to say that the fruit of doing a commandment is doing another commandment; and he eats its fruits in this world, which is that it helps him to do other commandments. And it comes out that the principle expands and it exists in the world to come. And this is what is stated - "Hail the just man, for he is good; they shall eat the fruit of their works".

And the reward for a sin is another sin: And if he chose death and evil and did a sin, the Holy One, blessed be He, distances Himself from him and leaves him and gives him over to his evil nature. And this is the fruit that comes out of the sin - that he is left to do another sin, and he does not have the ability to veer from this path; as a man's path is not his own once he has already chosen his path. And this is what is stated - "Woe to the evil wicked man; as his hands have dealt, so shall it be done to him." And about this the rabbis, may their memory be blessed, said - "One who comes to purify himself is helped; one who comes to defile himself is given openings." That is to say that if he comes to defile himself, he is not helped; but has many openings in which to enter and do evil - as he is left to do what is good in his own eyes. And about this the sages, may their memory be blessed, gave a parable - To what is this similar? To a man buying petroleum [Naphtha]. When he comes, the seller says to him, "Measure for yourself" as if he did not buy it with his money, he would not have permission to touch it. But after they sold it, he says to him, "Measure for yourself" because its smell is bad. So, is it with the evildoers; after they have chosen the path of evil, they are left to their desire and their will? As, God forbid that it be otherwise no man is assisted from the Heavens for a bad thing. But the righteous who choose the good path are assisted for the good. There is a parable [relevant to this] of a man who bought fragrant oil [Afarsimon]. When he went to measure it for himself, they said to him, "Wait until we measure it with you, and we will all be perfumed from it.

3. He used to say: do not despise any man, and do not discriminate against anything, for there is no man that has not his hour, and there is no thing that has not its place.

Rabbeinu Yonah

He would say: Do not disparage anyone, and do not shun any thing: That you should not disparage any person, and even a lowly one. And do not exaggerate your words, to say that it is far removed that damage will come to me from this talk.

For you have no man who does not have his hour: Who is then able to damage or benefit - if little, if much.

And you have no thing that does not have its place: And so, you have to be careful about it.

4. Rabbi Levitas a man of Yavneh said: be exceeding humble spirit, for the end of man is the worm. Rabbi Yohanan ben Berokah said: whoever profanes the name of heaven in secret, he shall be punished in the open. Unwittingly or wittingly, it is all one in profaning the name.

Rabbeinu Yonah

Rabbi Levitas, a man of Yavneh, says: Be very, very humble in spirit, for the hope of man is worms: How can a man be proud at all as in the end, the worms will be better than he? And about this he said, "Be very, very humble in spirit" to emphasize the thing and say how great the punishment is for haughtiness and that is the proud one. And Rambam, may his memory be blessed, explained that he came to inform us that even though the middle point in all of the traits is the praiseworthy like the trait of generosity, since both the spendthrift and the miser are bad and the middle is the [right] choice; and so with the trait of cruelty, that a person should not be cruel and also not completely merciful, as he should not have mercy on the wicked, and not be cruel to other people, rather the middle is the good path, to be merciful but to be cruel when needed; and so too totally with all the traits, a man should grab the middle path and the moderate trait yet this trait of haughtiness must be removed from oneself to the far extreme. As there is no trait more problematic than it; and most of the sins of the Torah depend upon it. And moreover, it causes forgetfulness of the Creator, may He be blessed, from the heart of a man - as it is stated - "And your heart grow haughty and you forget the Lord, your God." And this is what we learned here, "Be very, very humble in spirit." And the sages of the Talmud have already argued about this thing - "One said, In excommunication is the one that has it and in excommunication is the one that does not have it at all." This is to say that a person should not be humble in spirit to the final extreme and not to be so lowly that people disparage him. Rather, he should be moderate in taking haughtiness - not to make himself proud, but not to lower his spirit to the utmost lowliness, that he not come to disgrace. And about this they said, "In excommunication is the one that has" much haughtiness "and in excommunication is the one that does not have it at all" - as he is not a person, but he is similar to the beasts. "And the other one said, In excommunication is the one that has it at all" as it is so bad a trait that he must distance himself from it completely. And there should not be in him from it at all, like the opinion of Rabbi Levitas, and for the reason that we have written. And so is the law.

Rabbi Yochanan ben Beroka says: Anyone who desecrates the Name of Heaven secretly, they punish him publicly: Of course, the desecration of the Name that is mentioned in the Talmud is public by definition. And according to the importance of a man can there be a desecration for a small thing, as was said by Rav Nachman - "How is desecration of the Name? Rav said, For example, if I took meat from the butcher and did not give him money immediately." Hence the sages and men of repute need to watch their deeds more than other people. And every man is according to his standing. And anyone who wants to take the name, and consider himself important in this regard, let him come and take [it].' And they said - that even for tying a shoelace, in the way of the gentiles, he should let himself be killed and not transgress. This is not by way of obligation, yet one should let himself be killed for this - as he is doing a commandment that sanctifies God, may He be blessed, and so he acquires his share in the world to come in an instant. But in three things everyone is obligated to let himself be killed for them; and if he transgresses and does not allow himself to be killed, it is a major sin in itself like idolatry, murder and sexual immorality. And the punishment for public desecration of the Name is greater than those three, as it is stated - "As for you, House of Israel, thus said the Lord God, Go, every one of you, and worship his idols and continue, if you will not obey Me; but do not desecrate My holy name any more with your idols and your gifts." Behold, it is elucidated for you that He was more, in remembrance of, exacting about that which they were worshiping idols because they were desecrating His holy Name publicly than because of the idolatry itself. And hence that which we learned, "Anyone who desecrates the Name of Heaven secretly," is speaking about things that are a desecration of the Name in of themselves, like idolatry as he is affirming **the idol's** divinity. And so too, the one who swears falsely with the Name of the Holy One, blessed be He which is deceiving the minds of the creatures - is a desecration - as it is stated - "You shall not swear falsely by My Name, desecrating the Name of your God; I am the Lord."

There is no differentiation between unintentional and intentional when it comes to desecration of the Name: Not that he is punished for the unintentional like the intentional; but rather that also for the unintentional is he punished publicly, and each one will carry the punishment according to his transgression. This is because the unintentional is considered a transgression in such a case when it is not beyond his control, since he should have been careful that it not come to him - and he was not careful. Therefore, the verse obligates him in a sacrifice in order to atone for him.

5. Rabbi Ishmael his son said: He who learns in order to teach, it is granted to him to study and to teach; But he who learns in order to practice, it is granted to him to learn and to teach and to practice. Rabbi Zadok said: do not make them a crown for self-exaltation, nor a spade with which to dig. So too Hillel used to say, "And he that puts the crown to his own use shall perish." Thus, you have learned, anyone who derives worldly benefit from the words of the Torah, removes his life from the world.

Rabbeinu Yonah

Rabbi Yishmael his son, says: One who studies Torah in order to teach: The explanation is not, God forbid, that this is speaking about studying in order to teach and not to do - since such a one is given into his hand neither to learn nor to teach. Rather it is in order to do according to that which is forbidden and that which is permissible, and not to toil and look into it much; as maybe he will find something forbidden in the permissible things. Instead, he takes things according to their simple meaning. Because of that, he will only "be given the opportunity" according to his thought, which is to study and to teach.

One who studies in order to practice will be given the opportunity to study, to teach and to practice: He wants to say that his intention is to analyze his learning so as to know the truth of the matters and his will is to toil several days and [even] years to fathom a small thing and to conduct himself according to the truth; behold, this is one who studied in order to practice - as the whole thrust of his intent is only that his action be truthful. Therefore, he "will be given the opportunity to study, to teach and to practice" - as it is all included in action.

Rabbi Tzadok says: Do not make it [the Torah] into a

crown with which to aggrandize yourself, and not into a spade: That he not makes his words of Torah like a spade to aggrandize himself and be honored on their account in this world, as that is benefit from honor. The exception is if he has the intention that if be for the Torah's honor. As when they show him honor, the Torah is honored by it. And if the whole-hearted intention of the sage is for the honor of the Torah - and not for his honor - it is permitted.

And not into a spade with which to dig into them: That he not have benefit of money, as one should not benefit from them at all.

And thus, Hillel used to say: And one who makes use of the crown taga of learning passes away: Taga is an expression that means crown, as crown is rendered in its classical Aramaic translation.

From here you learn that any one who benefits from the words of the Torah: One who benefits from words of Torah in this world, behold he **removes his life from the world** to come. And it is not only benefit from honor and benefit of money that they spoke about, but it is forbidden even to save oneself with Torah. As behold, they tied up Rabbi Tarfon to throw him into the river, as they thought that he was a thief. And he only said, "Woe to Tarfon, as this one is killing him." And since they then recognized that he was Rabbi Tarfon, they let him go and he ran away. All of the days of that righteous one, he was anguished about this thing and said, "Woe is to me that I have made use of the crown of Torah" - since anyone who makes use of the crown of Torah does not have a portion in the world to come. And we say the reason is because Rabbi Tarfon was very rich and he could have appeased him with money - And we also say - that Rabbi [**Rabbi Yehuda Hanassi**] opened his storehouses in a year of drought. He said, "Let the masters of scripture, the masters of Mishnah and the masters of Talmud enter! Let the ignoramuses not enter!" Rabbi Yochanan ben Amram pushed and entered; he said, "Rabbi, sustain me." He said [back] to him, "Have you read scripture?" "No." "Have you studied mishnah?" "No." "And if so, with in the merit of what should I sustain you?" He said, "Sustain me like a dog or a raven." He got up and sustained him. But after he left, he said, "Woe to me, since I gave from my money to an ignoramus." Rabbi Shimon be Rabbi said to him, "Maybe that was Yonatan ben Amram, your student, who does not want to benefit, with the honor, from the honor of Torah." They checked and found that it was like his words. Hence, Rabbi said, "Let all enter!" But didn't Rabbi also say he wanted to sustain based on the honor of Torah? Rather it was a year of drought, when it is a commandment to sustain whoever is lacking his needs; and the one who needs may take. However, Rabbi did not want to give benefit from his money to ignoramuses. And Rabbi followed his reasoning, as Rabbi said, "Punishment only comes to the world because of ignoramuses." And nonetheless Yonatan ben Amram went beyond the letter of the law. As since he saw that they were only sustaining Torah masters, he said, "If so, they are sustaining based on the honor of Torah" - and he did not want to benefit from the honor of Torah. And it appears that maybe if they had not been willing to sustain him on the condition that he was an ignoramus, he would have sustained himself through the honor of Torah - as this transgression is no greater than all of the commandments in the Torah, about which it is stated - "and live by them" and not that he die by them, except for the three known ones. And that which they said - "From here, we see that the verse counts one who brings a gift to Torah scholars as if he brings up the first fruits" - they only said it about something to which commoners are also accustomed, as it is the way of people to bring a gift to an important person even if he is an ignoramus. And that which the sages said - "A scholar who wants to benefit, he may benefit like Elisha" - this is referring to one who puts his merchandise into the 'pocket' of Torah scholars, for them to resell for a profit, their reward for which is great and it is permissible. And the verse also exempts them from types of taxes and fees and even from money for the poll tax, and other benefits that are known from tradition that the Holy One, blessed be He, allowed Torah scholars. And so, did Rabbi Meir Halevi, may his memory be blessed, arrange the matter.

Pirkei Avot - Rabbeinu Yonah - Chapter 4

6. Rabbi Yose said: whoever honors the Torah is himself honored by others, and whoever dishonors the Torah is himself dishonored by others.

Rabbeinu Yonah

Rabbi Yosi says: Anyone who honors the Torah, etc.: And what is the honor of Torah? That he not place holy books on the floor, and that he not sit on a chair or bench together with them on the same level; and that he honors it and its learners. As it is a known thing by force of the verses and logic attest to it, that we can assume that someone who speaks well about the good and about the sages is righteous. And regarding any one who judges them unfavorably, takes up their actions to say that they are not thought out and does not see them to be a merit for them; and when evildoers are spoken about, he justifies their deeds, it is known that he has a trace of evil. And do not have a doubt that you can discern the hearts of men by this. And there is a whole verse about this that Shlomo, peace be upon him, stated - "For silver, the crucible; for gold, the furnace; and a man, according to his praising" - meaning to say, according to what he praises. And even though it is written - "but the Lord sees to the heart," that is speaking concerning heresy. As a man does not have the ability to discern if his fellow is a heretic, since these are matters hidden in the hearts of the heretics. But the speech of the believers "but they are like believers in their speech."

His body will be honored by the created beings: He is helped from the Heavens that the created beings will honor him, since he honors the Torah and does the things that we mentioned. And about their opposites, they said:

Anyone who desecrates the Torah, his body will be desecrated by the created beings: About these they said, one who reveals [improper] faces of the Torah and says, "Why was it necessary to write - And Timna was a concubine?" and similar to it - behold this is one who desecrates the Torah.

7. Rabbi Ishmael his son said: he who refrains himself from judgment, rids himself of enmity, robbery and false swearing; But he whose heart is presumptuous in giving a judicial decision, is foolish, wicked and arrogant.

Rabbeinu Yonah

Rabbi Yishmael, his son, says: One who withholds himself from judging: Even though it is written - "You shall appoint magistrates and officials in all of your gates," and - "Justice, justice shall you pursue," as it is a commandment to judge legal cases - that is in a place where there are no other judges. But any time he can withhold himself, it is good for him to send its yoke onto others, since that way he will prevent himself from several problems.

Removes from himself enmity: As one who leaves the court guilty will hate the judges.

Theft: Lest he obligate one who is not guilty to pay; and the matter is considered for him as if he had stolen from him.

And the false oath: Lest they obligate one an oath that is not according to the law; and it comes out that he makes him stumble in a vain oath.

One who is nonchalant about giving legal decisions: He put this thing adjacent to the one who withholds himself from judging because the latter needs to decide upon it with deliberation and much analysis and so the matter is a burden to him; but in contrast the one who is nonchalant about giving legal decisions that thinks about himself that he knows to give the correct legal decisions and he will not err:

Is an imbecile: He is called an imbecile because he is wise in his own eyes, and there is no greater imbecility than this -

as there is more hope for a fool than for him. Since when the fool does sins, he himself knows and recognizes that he is not walking on the good path, and he does not think that he is not erring. And so, there is hope for his betterment, as maybe he will repent to God. But with the wise one in his own eyes who is nonchalant about giving legal decisions, what hope is there? Since he thinks that he is wise, how will he change - as it would appear to him like leaving wisdom and intelligence.

wicked: Even though he already said that he is an imbecile, that expression does not include his not being a fearer of sin. Because of this, he needed to say that he is also wicked. As if he had fear of Heaven, he would not have been so quick with his words - since he knows, that comprehension, that error is found among people and it is easy for any person to sin, and even for the greatest and most analytical sage.

And arrogant in spirit: Even though he already said that he is imbecile and does not fear sin, now he adds and says that it is from haughtiness and arrogance of spirit and from wanting to lord it over others that he is nonchalant about giving legal decisions it is in order that the world see that he decides legal cases quickly and to show them that he is wise, so they will appoint him to be a judge and master over them. And that is his evil thought. Behold, these three traits are in the one who is nonchalant about giving legal decisions and who renders [these] decisions without trepidation and fear may the Omnipresent, in His mercy, save us from them.

8. He used to say: judge not alone, for none may judge alone save one. And say not "accept my view", for they are free but not you.

Rabbeinu Yonah

He would say: Do not judge alone: This is also from the matter of withholding oneself from judging. As even though an expert, judges, even alone, it is of the trait of piety that he not do so but wait until he takes colleagues that judge with him and they will help him. And it comes out a little that he withholds himself from judging, as not all of the judging is placed upon him.

For there is no lone judge aside from One - God: He wants to say that there is no lone judge except for the Holy One, blessed be He. And there is someone who explains, "for there is no lone judge aside from one" that this is the expert, but not other people who are not experts. And therefore, a person should not consider himself an expert and he should think that he needs a group.

And do not say, "Accept my opinion": Also, when you take a group to judge the legal case and they disagree with you, do not say, "I am the expert and they are not experts. Hence they should accept my opinion and nullify their opinions in my favor. As if it were not for my humility, I would have judged the case alone; so now too, decide according to my argument." As you should not think this.

For they are permitted and not you: If your colleagues agree with your opinion, it is upon them to accept your words. But, if not, you are not permitted to force them about this.

9. Rabbi Jonathan said: whoever fulfills the Torah out of a state of poverty, his end will be to fulfill it out of a state of wealth; And whoever discards the Torah out of a state of wealth, his end will be to discard it out of a state of poverty.

Rabbeinu Yonah

Rabbi Yonatan says: Anyone who implements the Torah in poverty: Since he compresses his hours and neglects his work needed for his livelihood in order to implement the Torah and the commandment, and so he studies and does the commandments in difficulty:

his end will be to implement it in wealth: As he will become wealthy, And in addition, he will also have broad hours to be occupied with Torah study and to implement the commandments, since his income will be great. And he will not require the toil of his hands, but rather he will eat and study in joy and with a good heart. As through wisdom, he will have all the good. It is as we found with King Shlomo, peace be upon him, who asked for wisdom and did not ask for silver and gold, as it is stated - "Keep lies and false words far from me; give me neither poverty nor riches, but provide me with my daily bread." There is a parable relevant to this about a king that said to his servant, "Ask for what I should give you." The servant said, "If I ask for silver and gold, he will give it to me; for properties and lands, he will give it to me. I will ask for the king's daughter for my wife, and everything else will be included." So did Shlomo, peace be upon him, say -"I will ask for wisdom and everything else is included, For to be in the shelter of wisdom is to be in the shelter of money".

And anyone that disregards the Torah in wealth: Since many times and many hours, he had the free time to study and did not do it, he:

Will in the end disregard it in poverty: As he will need to exert himself for his livelihood and he will not find it; to the point that, as poetic justice, he will not find free time to be occupied with Torah, even if he wanted. And it comes out that he will leave the world without Torah.

10. Rabbi Meir said: Engage but little in business, and busy yourself with the Torah. Be of humble spirit before all men. If you have neglected the Torah, you shall have many who bring you to neglect it, but if you have labored at the study of Torah, there is much reward to give unto you.

<u>Rabbeinu Yonah</u>

Rabbi Meir says: Minimize business and engage in Torah: That you make your work flexible, and your Torah fixed.

Be humble of spirit before everyone: This thing is also from the topic of Torah, and so it was said in the midst of his words that were words about Torah and he did not put it earlier nor later. And he wanted to say that even if you are successful in Torah study, which is the true advantage do not become haughty; and it is not necessary to say that it is not fit to become haughty for all of the other foreign, physical advantages.

Be humble of spirit before everyone: And even before the lowly and the degraded and the inferior, so as to distance oneself from the trait of haughtiness, and it is not necessary to say, before one that is your equal.

If you neglect the Torah, many reasons for neglecting it will be presented to you: These are the evildoers, the bears and the lions, that bring neglect from work, as they are the disciplining staff. And through them the Holy One, blessed be He, punishes those neglectful of Torah study. As He does not want to pay back with His own hand, but rather through others - with the trait of punishment.

And if you labor in Torah, He God has abundant reward to grant you: The Holy One, blessed be He, Himself in the

Pirkei Avot - Rabbeinu Yonah - Chapter 4

His full glory gives the reward for those that are occupied with His Torah - not through an angel and not through a messenger. And with this He is assuring all of those that come to the world that He sends the punishments through His messengers to lighten the matter, as not like our Rock is their rock. But great peace is there to those who love His Torah, and goodly reward to those that fear Him. He pays them by His hand and not through others, in order to increase their reward. There is a parable relevant and to this about a king for whom a craftsman made a fine vessel. The king commanded and said to his servants that they should take money from his treasury and pay him nicely. And will they not give him less than if the king himself would pay him? As their hearts are not broad like the heart of the king, due to his great wealth and honor; and their nature towards generosity is not like his nature. Even if they give the king's money, their present will be smaller than the king's present. So too is, the blessed Holy One, blessed be He, in the trait of goodness. He wants to give with His hand to enlarge the reward and elevate it.

11. Rabbi Eliezer ben Jacob said: he who performs one commandment acquires for himself one advocate, and he who commits one transgression acquires for himself one accuser. Repentance and good deeds are a shield against punishment. Rabbi Yochanan Hasandlar said: every assembly which is for the sake of heaven, will in the end endure; and every assembly which is not for the sake of heaven, will not endure in the end.

Rabbeinu Yonah

Rabbi Eliezer ben Yaakov says: One who does a single commandment acquires a single defender: That is one that advises good for a person in front of the king.

One who does a single sin acquires a single prosecutor: That is one that advises bad for a person in front of the king.

Repentance and good deeds are like a shield against punishment: As the repentance that a person does for his bad deeds and the good deeds that he did from the beginning behold, they protect him like a shield against punishment.

Rabbi Yochanan the shoemaker says: Every gathering that is for the sake of Heaven, its end is to endure: If it is for Torah or good deeds, it is called a gathering that is for the sake of Heaven.

And every gathering that is not for the sake of Heaven, its end is not to endure: This is when they gather, one to lord over the other, and each one seeks honor over his fellow.

12. Rabbi Elazar ben Shammua said: let the honor of your student be as dear to you as your own, and the honor of your colleague as the reverence for your teacher, and the reverence for your teacher as the reverence of heaven.

Rabbeinu Yonah

Rabbi Elazar ben Shamua says: Let the honor of your student be dear to you as your own, like the honor of your fellow: He wants to say each one according to his honor, that is known to be fitting for his fellow and for a student respectively. But he is not saying that he honors his student like his fellow, as this is not correct. But rather just like you are not allowed to subtract from the honor of your fellow that is fitting for him, so too do you not have the right to lessen from the honor that is fit for your student.

And the honor of your fellow like the reverence of your teacher, and the reverence of your teacher like the reverence of Heaven: Honor is included in reverence, but reverence is not included in honor, as Malakhi stated - "A son should honor his father, and a slave his master; and if I am a father, where is My honor, yet if I am a master, where is My reverence, etc.?" - he said **fear** with a slave, and **honor** with a son, as the matter is like this. And here, it mentioned fear for the teacher and for Heaven, as one needs to fear teachers, because fear of the teacher is the foundation of fear of Heaven. This is since he teaches him Torah and to fear the Lord, his God. And one who loves the Torah, loves the sages and will fear the word of God. And to the one who teaches him, there is within him the fear of Heaven and walking in the good path, that is why it says, "the reverence of your teacher." But with the student and the fellow it only mentioned honor, as one is not obligated in their reverence. It comes out that you have learned that the honor of your student needs to be as dear in your eyes as the reverence of

Heaven, that is incumbent upon you. And you may not negate the one, just like the other, as they are all dependent, one upon the other. And, if so, the four of them are all of one level - the honor, according to the honor of each; and the reverence, according to the reverence, of each.

13. Rabbi Judah said: be careful in study, for an error in study counts as deliberate sin. Rabbi Shimon said: There are three crowns: the crown of torah, the crown of priesthood, and the crown of royalty, but the crown of a good name supersedes them all.

Rabbeinu Yonah

Rabbi Yehuda says: Be careful in study, for an error in study is considered an intentional transgression: As he should review the things until he can not forget anything, and to the point that he reaches the depths of the matters, since the nature of a man is short in understanding wisdom and since forgetfulness is common among people. He should also not rely upon his first reasoning, as we wrote at the beginning of the book. As with all this he is committing an intentional transgression, since in anything that is a matter of the Torah and of the commandment wherein error is common and he still does not pay attention to it and errs, he is not accidental, but rather he is called a transgressor [Poshea]. As he should have thought that every man errs and have been careful not to sin, but he was not careful. And there are four relevant categories: the transgressor, the one close to being an intentional transgressor, the accidental sinner and the one close to being under duress, out of his control.

Rabbi Shimon says: There are three crowns: the crown of Torah, the crown of priesthood and the crown of monarchy: The crown of priesthood was given to the House of Aharon, as it is stated - "It shall be for him and his descendants after him a pact of priesthood for all time." And the crown of monarchy was given to the House of David, as it is stated - "His seed shall be forever; his throne, as the sun before Me." But the crown of Torah rests available for all those that come to the world, one who wants to merit it, let him come and merit. And this crown is greater than the other two crowns, as the rabbis, may their memory be blessed, said

- "There are three decorative rims: he rim of the table, the rim of the inner altar and the rim of the cover on top of the ark, in which rests the Torah, engraved upon the tablets. And the cover and its rim rests inside the dividing curtain, whereas the other two rest outside the dividing curtain. Behold for you that the Torah is more glorious than the table that corresponds to the table of the kings; and likewise [than] the altar that is the crown of priesthood, since they burn incense upon it every day." And there is another proof. That is that there are houses for monarchy and priesthood: a house for monarchy, as it is stated - "House of David, thus said the Lord, Decide justice in the morning"; a house for priesthood, as it is stated - "House of Aharon... House of Levi." But for fear of God, which is the crown of Torah, there is no special house, as it is stated - "those who fear the Lord, bless the Lord" - "in every place where I cause My name to be mentioned I will come to you and bless you."

But the crown of a good name outweighs - rises above them all: He wants to say that for all of the crowns, they need the crown of a good name. And behold, that is dependent upon the crown of Torah. For with what is there a good name to a man if not because he is occupied in Torah study and fulfills the commandments? And about this is it stated -"A good name is better than good oil." He meant to say here that if he puts down afarsimon oil in his house, it has a good smell for him and for the people of his house and for his close neighbors. But if they distance themselves from it a little, they do not smell it. But with one who is crowned by a good name - even if he stands in this corner, his reputation goes from one end of the world to the other. "And the day of death than the day of his birth." Here he wanted to say as from the good name has more significance than the good oil, so too is the day of death more significant than the day of his birth for someone who departs with a good name. And if people are happy about the birth and sad on the day of death, it is because they do not have understanding. There is a parable relevant to this about a city with a ship leaving the sea for dry land and a ship entering the sea from dry land: For the one entering the sea they make music and parties, but for the one leaving it, they don't do anything at all. And are the people of this city not fools? As at the time that it is entering the danger of the sea, they should have been afraid for it and not rejoice; and when it left and was saved from the great danger, it would have been fitting to make music and to rejoice. So too when a person is born is it fitting to be afraid for him, as to whether he will go on the good path or whether he will not. But when he leaves with a good name from the world, [it is fitting that] his neighbors and friends will rejoice for him. But they do the opposite.

Rabbi Meir said: Make His will like your will, etc.: We have already explained it in the second chapter, with the help of Heaven.

Pirkei Avot - Rabbeinu Yonah - Chapter 4

14. Rabbi Nehorai said: go as a [voluntary] exile to a place of Torah and say not that it will come after you, for [it is] your fellow [student]s who will make it permanent in your hand and "and lean not upon your own understanding".

Rabbeinu Yonah

Rabbi Nehorai says: Exile yourself to a place of Torah: That you should live in a place that has much Torah, and many sages in it.

And do not say that it will follow after you, that your colleagues will make it yours: Do not rely upon your colleagues that went to study, that they will come and teach you. As you, yourself, need to exile yourself with them and to pursue the Torah if you want to know it.

Do not rely on your understanding: Even when you do study and exile yourself to a place of Torah and become wise, "do not rely on your understanding" that you not depend upon your rationale; but rather you should do all of the deed according to the counsel of the sages.

15. Rabbi Yannai said: it is not in our hands to explain the reason either of the security of the wicked, or even of the afflictions of the righteous. Rabbi Mathia ben Harash said: Upon meeting people, be the first to extend greetings; And be a tail unto lions, and not a head unto foxes.

Rabbeinu Yonah

Rabbi Yanai says: We do not have the tranquility of the wicked: As the righteous do not have the quiet and security and wealth and all the needs of the world, like the wicked.

Or even the suffering of the righteous: The afflictions of love of the righteous, in such a way that they will not be prevented from Torah study. And there are some that explain, "We do not have the tranquility of the wicked," that even though it is just that the wicked has it good and the righteous suffers, nonetheless we do not grasp the reason of the thing. And it is from the truths the argument for which our knowledge does not grasp. And this is what Yirmiyah, peace be upon him, said - "You are correct, Lord, if I argue upon You; yet I shall present cases with You: Why does the way of the wicked prosper; are the workers of treachery at ease?" And about this is it said, "We do not have the tranquility of the wicked" - since we know that there is truthfully an argument for the matter, but we do not grasp to know it.

Rabbi Mattia ben Charash says: Be the first to greet every person: And this is from the ethical path.

And be a tail to lions: He wants to say that one should service Torah scholars and cling to their company.

And do not be a head to foxes: This is saying to you that it is better for a man to be a student to someone greater than him in wisdom, since it will come out that he will be adding to his wisdom every day; than to be the master of someone lesser than he in wisdom, as it will come out that they will continually lessen in his wisdom. It is as they said, "One who was the head of a lower court is made secondary to the high court." Another explanation: "and do not be a head to foxes" - that he should not be a head and a minister and an officer to the wicked. And this is what Shlomo, peace be upon him, stated - "He who walks with the wise becomes wise; he who consorts roeh with dullards will be broken." He wanted to say that the one who walks with the wise - to be lowly [towards them] - becomes wise; as he makes himself "a tail to lions." But one who consorts with dullards - that he becomes a lord over them, since a roeh, which also means shepherd, is a head will be broken.

16. Rabbi Jacob said: this world is like a vestibule before the world to come; prepare yourself in the vestibule, so that you may enter the banqueting-hall.

Rabbeinu Yonah

Rabbi Yaakov says: This world is like a hallway before the world to come. Fix yourself in the hallway so you may enter the beautiful traklin: A traklin is a palace, And he wants to say that this world is only in order that one should merit the world to come.

17. He used to say: more precious is one hour in repentance and good deeds in this world, than all the life of the world to come; And more precious is one hour of the tranquility of the world to come, than all the life of this world.

Rabbeinu Yonah

He would say: One hour of repentance and good deeds in this world is better than all the time in the world to come: As in a short time in this world, a person can earn the world to come - as we find - that story about Yosi ben Yoezer who was going out to be killed and he was met by the wicked Yokim, the man of Tsrorot, riding on a horse: The latter said to the former, "Look at the horse that your Master made you ride and look at the horse that our master made us ride." He said back to him, "If it is thus for those that transgress His will, is it not all the more so for those that do His will?" And he responded in turn, "Is there any one that is more of one who does His will than you?" He said back, "If it is like this for those who do His will, even more so will it be for those who transgress His will." This went into his heart like fire into chaff - the explanation is that he understood from his words when he said, "If things are so good for the wicked who transgress His will in this world, all the more so will it be so for the righteous in the world to come," that it will be doubly and exponentially better than the good of the wicked in this world. And that there, there is no peace for the wicked, as it will be twice as bad for them than for the righteous in this world. And when he heard this, he went and accepted upon himself the four death penalties of the court, etc., as it is found over there. Rabbi Yosi ben Yoezer said, "In a short time, he preceded me [passed me by] to the Garden of Eden." And about this, it is said, "Better is one hour, etc." And only about this did he praise this world. Also, King Shlomo who scared who considered vain the world in his book Kohelet, yet in a few places he praises the living over the dead - also that praise is only about repentance and good deeds. As they raise a person up in this world, but not in the world to come since a person is only finally judged at the time of his death.

And one hour of pleasure in the world to come is better than all the time in this world: As the rabbis, may their memory be blessed, said - "All of the prophets only prophesied with regard to the messianic era; however, with regard to the world to come it was stated. No eye sees, God, except You, that which He will do for he that waits for Him as the good of the world to come has neither measure not comparison. And this is what David, peace be upon him, said - "How abundant is the good that You have in store for those who fear You, that You do in front of men for those who take refuge in You." May the Omnipresent let us merit it.

18. Rabbi Shimon ben Elazar said: Do not try to appease your friend during his hour of anger; Nor comfort him at the hour while his dead still lies before him; Nor question him at the hour of his vow; Nor strive to see him in the hour of his disgrace.

Rabbeinu Yonah

Rabbi Shimon ben Elazar says: Do not assuage the anger of your friend at the time of his anger: As through this, he will come to say inappropriate things about him, as he will add anger to his anger.

Do not console him at the time when his deceased lies before him: As at the time of sadness, consolation brings anger to him, and he will come to say things that are not good.

Do not question him at the time of his vow: That he should not ask him about all the openings of permission that can be used later to annul the vow to say, "Did you vow with this intention?" As when he is still angry and making the vow, he will come to express all of the questions that they ask him and place them into the wording of the vow in such a way that no opening will be able to be found for him. And it comes out that he causes him bad.

And do not seek to see him and to embarrass him also now at the time of his humiliation: at the time of the damage or if he did a sin and he is embarrassed about himself, you should not see him and embarrass him more.

19. Shmuel Hakatan said: "If your enemy falls, do not exult; if he trips, let your heart not rejoice, lest the Lord see it and be displeased, and avert his wrath from him."

Rabbeinu Yonah

Shmuel the Younger says: "When your enemy falls, do not be happy, and when he stumbles, let your heart not rejoice": And what does Shmuel come to let us hear with this - is it not a full verse that Shlomo stated? Rather, it wants to say that Shmuel was accustomed to saying this verse since it is something needed and people stumble in it. Since even when the enemy is wicked, one should not be happy in the bad that happens to him, except only for the sake of God. We want to say that this righteous one should not be happy in the fall of the wicked unless the intention of his joy is because his fall is a manifestation of God's glory, and not because of his hating him. And all the more so, one whose actions are corrupted like him - if the heart of [such a one] would rejoice in his stumbling, his evil is great. And why is he happy - behold, he is just like him! And about all this is it stated, "When your enemy falls, do not be happy, and when he stumbles, let your heart not rejoice." And Shmuel's intention in constantly saying it was about this. And there are those that follow the textual variant, "Lest God see and it be bad in His eyes and He turn from him the enemy His anger" - "burning anger" is not stated which is only the heat of anger, but rather "anger from upon him"; this teaches that he is forgiven for all of his sins: And now Shmuel is coming to let us hear a great novelty, as he wants to say that when God sees that this one is happy about the fall of his enemy, He forgives the enemy and rehabilitates him, and He punishes the one who is happy.

Pirkei Avot - Rabbeinu Yonah - Chapter 4

20. Elisha ben Abuyah said: He who learns when a child, to what is he compared? To ink written upon a new writing sheet. And he who learns when an old man, to what is he compared? To ink written on a rubbed writing sheet. Rabbi Yose ben Judah a man of Kfar Ha-babli said: He who learns from the young, to what is he compared? To one who eats unripe grapes, and drinks wine from his vat; And he who learns from the old, to what is he compared? To one who eats ripe grapes, and drinks old wine. Rabbi said: don't look at the container but at that which is in it: there is a new container full of old wine, and an old - container in which there is not even new wine.

Rabbeinu Yonah

Elisha ben Abuya says: One who teaches to a child is compared to what? To ink written on new parchment: As writing on new parchment cannot be erased, so too the Torah of his youth will not be forgotten from his heart.

And one who teaches to an elder is compared to what? To ink written on scraped parchment: As that writing will quickly be lost. So too is the Torah of his old age quickly forgotten. And there is a metaphor about this said in Choice Pearls: "One who teaches to a child is compared to what?" To one who engraves on a stone. "And one who teaches to an elder is compared" to one who engraves on the sand. But the elder should not say, "Behold I am a dry tree" - that since the Torah does not stay preserved in his hand, why should he read, and he would toil in vain - since nonetheless, his reward is with him for having learned and exerting himself and doing a commandment. And what difference is it to him if he does not remember it - whether it is this way or that way, he is given the reward. There is a parable [relevant to this] about an employer who gave containers with holes to two workers with which to draw water, and he agreed with them that they do this work for him for a day. The silly one said, "What is the point of my work?" The clever one said, "What is it to me? He will give me the wage [regardless]." So is [it with] the elder - what is to him if he forgets, the reward will be given to him. It is the same for the one who remembers a lot and the one who remembers a little - as long as his heart is directed to the Heavens.

Rabbi Yose ben Yehuda, man of Kfar HaBavli, says: One who learns from elders is compared to what? To one who eats ripe grapes and drinks aged wine: As by aging with the wisdom, each and every day he adds new faces to each and every thing and improves them; and he reaches the bottom of knowledge, to the point where it is easy for him to understand. As wisdom is with the seniors, and understanding with the long-lived.

And one who learns from young ones is compared to what? To one who eats unripe grapes and drinks wine from its press: As their wisdom has still not ripened within them.

Rebbi says: Do not look at the jug but rather at what is in it. For there are new jugs full of old, and old that do not have even new within them: As because of the quality of the old wine, it will not go bad in the new vessel. So too, if the young ones have become wiser than the elders. every man should learn from the younger ones first. And this is the difference between the words of Rabbi Yose ben Yehuda and the words of our holy Rabbi, peace be upon him: As Rabbi Yose would say that if the elders and the young ones are both wise, one should learn with the elders - since that the wisdom of the elders is ripe. And our Rabbi, peace be upon would say that with wisdom, we only go with the greater. And so, if it is found that the young ones are more understanding and their words are correct and their wisdom is greater, one should learn in front of them. And Elihou said both of these things, as it is stated - "I said, let age speak; let advanced years declare wisdom.' But truly it is the spirit in men, the breath of the Almighty that gives them understanding." As at first, he would say like the words of Rabbi Yose ben Yehuda - that "advanced years declare wisdom." But after he saw that he was younger than his colleagues, the elders, he said that "it is the spirit in men." And sometimes it is the young one who is wiser than the elder and his wisdom is riper than the latter. And his words are refined and the matters are clear. Hence, it is better to go after a young one who is wise than an elder who is honored but is not like the first in wisdom.

Pirkei Avot - Rabbeinu Yonah - Chapter 4

21. Rabbi Elazar Ha-kappar said: envy, lust and [the desire for] honor put a man out of the world.

Rabbeinu Yonah

Rabbi Elazar HaKapor says: Envy: The explanation regarding the matter of envy is that there are two things that have two or three matters, and two which are not harmful. The first way is envy of the good, and it is the worst way. And the first manner of this is that when his fellow sees good, it is bad in his eyes. And when the latter is occupied with Torah [study] and the commandments and goes in the good path, he begrudges him - as he hates those that love God and those that do His will. This trait drives him from the world and it is the greatest evil in envy. And his name is called the haters of God. And the second manner is that it is not bad in his eyes from the angle that he hates the path of involvement in Torah. Rather it is [that] since he does not walk in that path, he also does not want his fellow to go in it. As it is his will that no one find better than he - not for his benefit, but for the harm of others. This one is also called the haters of God - since he does not do the acts of God, it is also hard in his eyes to see his fellows doing [them], and even if he does not hate like the first. But there is a good path in envy, even if there is a better one. That is what the sages, may their memory be blessed, said -"The envy of scribes increases wisdom" - since by his seeing that his fellows are holy and wise, he also wants to be like them. And because of envy, he increases his wisdom and he toils and intensifies doing good and walking in the straight path. However, it is more valuable if he desires these without envy, as in that case they, are the speech of, are the ones that fear the Lord - and that is the work of man. And this is what King Shlomo, peace be upon, stated - "I have seen that all labor and skillful enterprise are from men's envy of each other; this too is vanity and broken spirit." He meant to say that even if he does an act skillfully; if he does it from envy of men, while he does good, there is also much bad. As one who does what is fitting from the generosity of his heart goes truthfully and with a full heart. Such a one is more worthwhile than the one who does it out of the envy of men when it comes to his heart. And if from this or from that, the act is done; 'but it is good for you to grasp the first without letting your hand go of the other. The second way is the envy of money. The first manner of this is the seeker of evil - and it is hard in his eyes that others have wealth, since he does not. And there is none in this way of envy as evil as this one - as he hates the good of the creatures and does not want the betterment of the world. And the second manner is one envious of his wealthy fellows; and it is hard in his eyes when they are wealthier than he. It is not from his hatred for them and for their wealth and that he desires that it be reduced. Rather, it is from his love of wealth and his desire to be very wealthy; since wealth is honor in his eyes, and he wants too more honored than they. And the third manner is the best of the bad ones - he loves money and is envious of it and desires that he should have great wealth. But he is not concerned if others have little or much. And this one's envy is not burning like the one that wants to be wealthier than all people. And King Shlomo, peace be upon him, grouped all of these things and stated - "Do not envy sinners in your heart, but only fear of the Lord all of the day." He first explained that the worst envy is not to be envious of the wicked that do sins, to do like them. And afterwards he stated more generally, "but only fear of the Lord" - all envies are negative except for the envy of fear of God. He should be envious of the acts of God, as He is awesome.

Lust, desire: It is the beginning of all activities and actions and is even before thought. As when he wants something from his desire for it, he thinks about doing it. And there is much bad in all desires. There is no need to say the desire of the impulse to sins, but even the desire for much permissible laying with women is very bad. And about this Sholmo, peace be upon him, stated - "Do not give your strength to women." And, so too, much desire for permissible food and drink - this too is bad. And it is like the wise men of science said, that even light and good foods are harmful to the one who eats much of them. And this is what they - "Do not accustom yourself to eat geese, as your heart will stalk you." And there are three bad ways of desire, just like with envy: The first is one who desires that there should not be wealth and honor to any other person, and that he should have them. And that is a transgression that he commits. And the second one desires for wealth and wisdom, but if others also have it, the thing is good in his eyes - except that he should have more than them, to be greater than them. There is also much bad in this. And in the third there is a little good. [It is the one] who when he sees that his fellows have wisdom and wealth, he desires that he should also be like them. And it is very good in his eyes that they be like him and God should add to them from Him a thousandfold and bless him and them. And this trait is not completely good, in that his desire is from the angle that others are wise and understanding and wealthy. As the fitting desire is to desire for wisdom from the angle that it is the foundation and root of service to the Creator, may He be blessed; and to do with the wealth that which is straight in the eyes of the Lord - and not because of any other thing. And this is what King David, peace be upon him, stated - "Lord, all my desire is in front of You." He wanted to say that all of his desire is from the angle of Heaven and from envy of men. And so too do we find with our holy Rabbi, peace be upon him - that at the time of his departure death, he raised his fingers and said - "It is revealed and known in front of You, Master of the worlds, that I have not enjoyed even the worth of a small finger." And even though our rabbis said about him - that he was very wealthy, such that his key carrier had like the wealth of Shavur Malka [the king of Persia], nonetheless Rabbi only enjoyed for the sake of Heaven, as he did not desire the vanities of the world.

And honor: The bad honor is practiced by the one who gets honor from people in order to impose his fear upon them and 'he strikes terror into the land of the living.' And what is his reward? That he will descend into the depths of the pit in

Gehinnom, such that there is no ascent form his fall for all generations. And because of this the prophet Yechezkel compares the fall of the kings of the nations in Gehinnom to the one who strikes terror into the land of the living,' to say that they have no ascent, as it is stated - "I strike My terror into the land of the living; and lay among the uncircumcised those who were the casualties of the sword." And the second way of honor is the one who wants that people should honor him, as he thinks that he is fit for this honor - but he is not. Even if he is a Torah scholar and a master of commandments and his will is that they honor him for this, he is 'sinning with his soul' - unless his intention is for the sake of Heaven, and if it is only for the honor of the Torah that he is seeking it and he does not take it for himself and does not enjoy it, but it is only in order to have the Torah honored about through this, as we have written. However, all other things regarding honor are very bad. And how much did the Torah warn and forbid it to them! As even with a king of Israel about whom it stated - "Surely place a king upon you" - that you should put his fear upon you, and so he is fit for honor more than all of the creatures under the skies, nonetheless it still warns him that he should not raise his heart over his brothers. All the more so should commoners not desire honor at all.

Drive a man from the world: As these three traits are in the category of major sins. Another explanation: "drive a man from the world" - **Envy**, as it is stated - And rot to the bones is envy"; **Lust**, as it is stated - "The lust of a lazy man kills him"; and **Honor**, as we have found with Yosef who died twelve years before his brothers, because he comported himself with lordship.

22. He used to say: the ones who were born are to die, and the ones who have died are to be brought to life, and the ones brought to life are to be judged; So that one may know, make known and have the knowledge that He is God, He is the designer, He is the creator, He is the discerner, He is the judge, He the witness, He the complainant, and that He will summon to judgment. Blessed be He, before Whom there is no iniquity, nor forgetting, nor respect of persons, nor taking of bribes, for all is His. And know that all is according to the reckoning. And let not your impulse assure thee that the grave is a place of refuge for you; for against your will were you formed, against your will were you born, against your will you live, against your will you will die, and against your will you will give an account and reckoning before the King of the kings of kings, the Holy One, blessed be He.

<u>Rabbeinu Yonah</u>

He would say: Those that are born will die: Since their end is to die, - and today alive, and tomorrow in the grave, they should contemplate their deeds and repent.

And those that are dead will be revived: As God, may He be blessed, will revive them in the future to come, as it is stated in Daniel - "And many of those that sleep in the dust of the earth will awake; these for eternal life, and those for reproaches, for everlasting abhorrence." Hence a man should do that thing such that he will be from the living and not from those who will experience everlasting abhorrence.

And the living will be judged: Those that will be revived in the future will stand in judgement in front of God, may He be blessed, and He will give them according to their activities and according to the actions of their hands.

It is necessary to know, to make known, and to become conscious: All need to know this. To know from others that will teach him; and to make known, that he should teach others in this world; and to be conscious in the world to come from himself without a teacher, as it is stated - "No longer will they teach a man his neighbor and a man say to his brother, Know the Lord; for all of them shall know Me, from the least of them to the greatest of them".

That He is God [E"l]: From the usage - "the strong ones **Eileh** of the land" meaning strong and resolute.

He is the Maker, He is the Creator: of the creatures from birth, from the womb and from inception. And making is the beginning of the act and creating is the end of the work. And it is not like the manufacturing of a vessel - as once it is finished, it does not require its manufacturer. But man requires their Creator at each instant and time, as King David, peace be upon him, said - "Know that the Lord is God; He made us and we are His, His people, the flock He tends." He wanted to say here that we need him every hour and minute.

He is the Understander: He understands all of their acts.

He is the Judge: Since He knows the truth of all matters, He is fit to judge, as He will judge the case truthfully.

He is the Witness: As everything is revealed in front of Him.

He is the Litigant: Since He is the one who makes the claim against the sinners, as David stated - "Against You alone have I sinned, and done what is evil in Your eyes; so, You are just in Your sentence, and right in Your judgment." As if a man hurt his fellow, he should not think that he has sinned to him and not to God, since He is the one that makes the claim of the damage, like a litigant - as he has also sinned to God.

And He is destined to judge: in the future to come.

Who has before Him no wrong: That He sway the judgement?

No forgetfulness, no respect of persons: That He forgive one who is great in wisdom and piety.

No taking of bribes: That He should deduct the reward from a commandment against the loss for a sin. Rather, he pays a goodly reward for the commandment and repays separately for the sin. And it is explained in Chronicles - that none of this is in front of Him.

And know that everything is according: to the reckoning whether for good or whether for bad.

And do not let your evil impulse assure you: To say to you that there is a place of refuge in the netherworld, as it appears to you that there is a place of refuge in this world - and like the heretics say, "In the world to come, there is neither judgement nor judge." Do not think and say this, as it is not true - because against your will you were created, and against your will you were born, and against your will you live, and against your will you die, and against your will you are destined to give account and reckoning before the King of kings, the Holy One, blessed be He.

Pirkei Avot - Rabbeinu Yonah - Chapter 4

Chapter 5

1. With ten utterances the world was created. And what does this teach, for surely it could have been created with one utterance? But this was so in order to punish the wicked who destroy the world that was created with ten utterances, and to give a good reward to the righteous who maintain the world that was created with ten utterances.

Rabbeinu Yonah

With ten utterances the world was created. And what is learned: "**And He said**" is written nine times from "In the beginning" to "And completed". And "In the beginning" is also an utterance, as it is stated - "By the word of the Lord the heavens were made" - as it is impossible that the heavens and the earth were created without an utterance.

And what is learned - couldn't it have been created by one utterance?: It wants to say, what is this teaching us, when it says, "With ten utterances the world was created?" Or the explanation is "what is learned" in creating it with ten utterances.

Rather, it is in order to punish the wicked. who destroy with their actions the world which is a big thing, as it **was created with ten utterances**, And the trait of strict justice will punish them accordingly in the future?

And to give reward to the righteous who sustain the world that was created with ten utterances: As the world was only created to do in it that which is straight in the eyes of the Lord. And hence those that do so, preserve it.

2. [There were] ten generations from Adam to Noah, in order to make known what long-suffering is His; for all those generations kept on provoking Him, until He brought upon them the waters of the flood. [There were] ten generations from Noah to Abraham, in order to make known what long-suffering is His; for all those generations kept on provoking Him, until Abraham, came and received the reward of all of them.

Rabbeinu Yonah

There were ten generations from Adam to Noah, to demonstrate the great extent of God's patience, for each one of those generations provoked God continually until God brought the waters of the flood upon them: And it comes to teach us that just like you see that in the generations between the first man **Adam** and **Noah**, all of them provoked Him with the action of their hands to cause bad to themselves and while He had great patience with all of those generations - in the end, He brought the waters of the flood upon them, as He is not greatly patient forever; so should you think about our exile. And that you not say, "How many days and years is it that He restrains His anger from upon the evil kingdom while we are in exile - He will have great patience towards them forever, as He is of great patience." And you should surely know that in the end, He will pay them back according to their activities and the action of their hands; and He will redeem us and save us. As even though His patience is very great; still in the end of days, He visits the first iniquities upon them, and may You quickly bring forward Your mercies, as we have become very poor.

There were ten generations from Noah to Abraham: And our rabbis said - "When Noah died, our father, Avraham was fifty-eight years old." Still, when you count the children you will find ten generations among them. As even if Noah had length of days, it is still considered ten generations.

to demonstrate the extent of God's patience, for each one of those generations provoked God continually, until Abraham came: And here they did not say, "until He punished them" as our father, Avraham, made up for all of their shortcomings and did good corresponding to all of their bad, and so he saved them from punishment. However, Noah was not able to save them, because he was not righteous enough to make up for their shortcomings.

And received the reward of them all: And even though there is a portion in the Garden of Eden and a portion in Gehinnom for every person - if he merits it, he takes his portion in the Garden of Eden; and if he is guilty in his judgement, he takes it in Gehinnom - nonetheless, since everyone is commanded to do good and this one does not do it and his fellow fulfills his commands and his own commands; the trait of justice would indicate that he should take his portion and the portion of his fellow in the Garden of Eden. And for this [reason] did our father, Avraham take the reward of all of them. And this is what is stated - "It is a time to act for the Lord, for they have violated Your Torah" - if you see a generation that is negligent from study of the Torah, be involved in it. And the simple meaning of the verse is "It is a time to act for the sake of the Lord." And similar to it is - "say for me, He is my brother" - which is like "for my sake." "They have violated your Torah" - since they are all violating Your Torah, I should do for the sake of the Lord more than in other generations, so that Torah is not, God forbid, forgotten in Israel. There is a parable relevant to this about a king whom all of his servants betrayed except for one. Does that servant not need to go with him truthfully and with a whole heart at that time more than other times? And so, all of his days the king will love him with a great love and increase his gift to be equal to the gifts of all of them together.

3. With ten trials was Abraham, our father (may he rest in peace), tried, and he withstood them all; to make known how great was the love of Abraham, our father (peace be upon him).

Rabbeinu Yonah

With ten tests Abraham, our father, was tested - and he withstood them all:
The first was Ur Kasdim - which besides being a place name can also mean fire, that Nimrod dropped him down into the fiery furnace and he was saved. And this is not explicit in the Torah and it is from the words of tradition. But we have a hint about this thing from the Torah; that before Parshat Lech Lecha Meartsekha ouMemoladetekha, Ur Kasdim is mentioned twice above it, to make known that it was because of that test that he withstood that God, may He be blessed, promised him and brought him to the land of Israel. This is like we find with Noah. As at the beginning it is written - "But Noah found favor in the eyes of the Lord," and afterwards in Parshat Eleh Toledot Noach that he was saved from the waters of the flood which indicates that it was because he found favor in his eyes.
And the second is that He commanded him to go out from his land and from his birthplace, and he did so.
And the third is that is stated - "And there was a famine in the land." And even though the Holy One, blessed be He, promised him and said to him - "And all the families of the earth shall bless themselves by you"; when He brought the famine, he did not question His traits.
The fourth is the taking of Sarah to Pharaoh.
The fifth is the war of the four kings when he deployed only three hundred and eighteen men and trusted in the Holy One, blessed be He; and a miracle was done for him that he was saved and he saved his brothers and all of the property of Sedom and Ammorah. And he endured the events accepting that it was for his good and for his merit.

The sixth is that he was ninety-nine when he circumcised the flesh of his foreskin and placed himself in danger due to his old age, and he was saved.

The seventh is the taking of Sarah to Avimelekh.

The eighth is when he sent Hagar and Yishmael away by the commandment of God. And even if the thing was bad in his eyes on account of his son, he fulfilled the commandment.

The ninth was the binding of Yitzchak his son, about which it is written - "For now I know that you fear God." And did He not know until now - and is not everything revealed and seen in front of Him? Rather when the thing is known to the creatures, the Holy One, blessed be He, calls it, "For now I know that you fear God." And it comes to inform us that this showed greater fear of Heaven than all of the other commandments in the Torah. Since with all the tests except for this, He did not say to him "that you fear God" - as this test was the greatest of all of them, since he took his son to bring him up as a sacrifice.

The tenth was the burial of Sarah. As it was stated to him - "Get up, walk about the land, through its length and its breadth, for I give it to you"; but when his wife died, he could not find a place to bury her until he bought it - and he did not question.

In order to show how great was the love of Abraham, our father: He tested him in order to reveal to the creatures that he feared God and was complete in all of his traits.

Pirkei Avot - Rabbeinu Yonah - Chapter 5

4. Ten miracles were wrought for our ancestors in Egypt, and ten at the sea. Ten plagues did the Holy one, blessed be He, bring upon the Egyptians in Egypt and ten at the sea. [With] ten trials did our ancestors try God, blessed be He, as it is said, "and they have tried Me these ten times and they have not listened to my voice".

Rabbeinu Yonah

Ten miracles were performed for our ancestors in Egypt: As our forefathers were not hurt by all of the ten plagues that the Holy One, blessed be He, brought on the Egyptians in Egypt. And it is explicit in all of them except the plague of lice, about which it is written -"And the lice were upon men" - and the Torah did not distinguish between Egypt and Israel. But it is a tradition in the hand of the sages that also with this [one] were they not struck.

And ten miracles were performed at the Reed Sea:
The first is the splitting of the Reed Sea, as it is stated - "and He opened the waters."
The second is that the water formed a bow and like a type of dome and it came out that the water was on top of them. And about this is it stated - "You have pierced with his rods, the head of his rulers."
The third is that the springs of the great foundations opened and absorbed all the moisture so that no mud or sludge remained on its ground, as is not the case when other springs dry up. Rather it was like marble stone on its bottom and so Israel crossed the sea as one who walks in his house.
The fourth is that the places that the Egyptians tread upon in the sea were like a type of clay, and this is what the verse states - "Your horses tread the sea, the clay of the mighty waters." It states "Your horses," as also the horses of the Egyptians were given into the hand of the Holy One, blessed be He.

Pirkei Avot - Rabbeinu Yonah - Chapter 5

And the fifth is that the waters hardened more than necessary and they became hard as boulders and slabs and hurt the Egyptians that were chasing Israel. And about this King David, peace be upon him, stated - "You smashed the heads of the sea monsters upon the waters" - these sea monsters were the Egyptians.

The sixth was that the waters were torn into twelve parts - one path for each tribe that would pass over there. And this is what is stated - "to tear the Reed Sea into many parts."

The seventh is that the partitions between one tribe and another were clear like white glass so that the tribes could see one another.

The eighth is that the water did not congeal into one piece, but rather it was made into many small pieces - like one block on top of another and one brick on top the other, as it is written - "You crumbled the sea with Your power."

The ninth is that the sweet fresh water did not harden like the rest of the waters of the sea but rather would flow; and they would drink from all of the streams going towards the sea.

The tenth is that after their drinking, the fresh water would immediately harden - as the flowing water would not descend to the floor. Rather, Israel would drink from it, and the rest would go out and fall to the ground like a piece of snow. And so too each and every time that they needed to drink.

Ten plagues did the Holy One, blessed be He, bring on the Egyptians in Egypt: These are the ten known by the acronym, Detsach, Adash, Beachav.

And ten at the sea:
The first, "and it lit the night" - and like the translation of Onkelos, "and it was darkness, cloud and fog for the Egyptians and light for Israel all night."

And the second and the third are "And the Lord looked down upon the Egyptian camp in a pillar of fire and cloud" - the cloud would come down and make it like sludge and the pillar of fire would boil it, such that the hoofs of their horses would be severed.

The fourth is "He removed the wheels of their chariots" - that He removed the wheels from the wagons and the Egyptians fell and were crushed.

The fifth is "and they drove with heaviness" - after they fell and were crushed, they could not stand. And so, they stayed in the place that they fell.

And the sixth is that they wanted to flee and they could not, as it is stated, "And Egypt said, Let us flee from Israel." And this is not like we found with Sisera, as it stated - "and Sisera descended from his chariot and fled on foot." But these did not descend and they did not have the possibility of fleeing.

And the seventh is "And the Lord shook the Egyptians into the sea" - likes its classic Aramaic translation, "and He confounded," which is an expression of breaking. As He shook them like a man shakes a pot, such that what is above goes below and what is below goes above.

And the eighth is that the earth at the bottom of the sea swallowed them, as it is stated - "You stretched out Your right hand, the earth swallowed them."

The ninth is that they descended heavily into the depths of the sea like lead, as it stated - "They sank like lead in the mighty waters."

The tenth is that the sea spit them out, as it stated - "And Israel saw Egypt dead on the shore of the sea".

With ten trials did our ancestors test the Omnipresent, blessed be He, in the Wilderness, as it is said - "Yet have they tested Me these ten times, and have not hearkened to My voice:"

The first is that they said - "Are there not enough graves in Egypt?"

And the second is - "And the people grumbled against Moses, saying, What shall we drink?" And a miracle happened that the Holy One, blessed be He, commanded Moshe to throw wood into the bitter waters, as it is stated - "And he cried out to the Lord, and the Lord showed him a piece of wood." And they said in Tractate Pesachim that this tree that the wood come from was a hardofanei, which is bitter. He threw bitter into bitter and it turned sweet.

The third was in the Wilderness of Sin when they asked for bread, as it stated - "when we sat over the fleshpot."

The fourth is - "Is the Lord amongst us or not?" There is a parable relevant to this about a man who carried his son on his shoulder; and the son was competent, but he said, "Have you seen Father?" What did his father do? He flung him from his shoulder. So did the Holy One, blessed be He, carry them on the wings of eagles - and yet they ask, "Is the Lord amongst us?" What did He do? He brought Amalek upon them.

The fifth is that they left manna over.

The sixth is that in Refidim they did not have water for the congregation.

The seventh was at Chorev with the story of the golden calf, as it is stated - "the people gathered against Aharon, etc."

The eighth was - "And the people were like grumblers of evil in the ears of the Lord." And He set a fire of the Lord against them and it consumed the edge of the camp, as the Lord, your God, is a consuming Fire, He is a jealous God.

The ninth was at the Graves of Desire [Kivrot HaTaavah] when they said - "Who will feed us meat?" And did they not have meat; and did they not have the quail at each and all times, as it is stated - "in that the Lord will give you meat to eat in the evening and bread in the morning to satiation." And just like the manna did not cease, the quail also did not cease. Rather they wanted meat in the evening to satiation, just like they had the bread. And about this our teacher Moshe, peace be upon him, stated, - "Could enough flocks and herds be slaughtered to suffice them, etc." Our teacher Moshe, peace be upon him said in front of the Holy One, blessed be He, "They have much meat; their request is only from the evil of their hearts. And since they are a stiff-necked people, even if You give them much more, they will continue to say there is not enough. Could enough flocks and herds be slaughtered - and their mouths will still not be satiated." The Holy One, blessed be He, said back to Him, "Is the hand of the Lord short? I will give them meat until they are satisfied and they will no longer be able to open their mouths to say, we are not satiated." And He added and brought them much more of the quails and they spread them all around and the least gathered ten chomer and they could not eat it all. Such is the simple meaning of the verse. And you will hence come to say that Moshe did not sin with his words. But our rabbis in the Talmud - did not interpret it thus.

And the tenth was in Midbar Paran when they sent the scouts. And there it states - "and they have tried Me these ten times".

5. Ten wonders were wrought for our ancestors in the Temple: **1.** no woman miscarried from the odor of the sacred flesh; **2.** the sacred flesh never became putrid; **3.** no fly was ever seen in the slaughterhouse; **4.** no emission occurred to the high priest on the Day of Atonement; **5.** the rains did not extinguish the fire of the woodpile; **6.** the wind did not prevail against the column of smoke; **7.** no defect was found in the omer, or in the two loaves, or in the showbread; **8.** the people stood pressed together, yet bowed down and had room enough; **9.** never did a serpent or a scorpion harm anyone in Jerusalem; **10.** and no man said to his fellow: the place is too congested for me to lodge overnight in Jerusalem.

Rabbeinu Yonah

Ten miracles were performed for our forefathers in the Temple: No woman had a miscarriage from the scent of the meat: that is on the outer altar and gives off a scent similar to any roast. And since is forbidden to derive benefit from holy meat, the Holy One, blessed be He, protected the women all of those days - that they should not have a miscarriage from that scent given they could not eat from it to prevent the miscarriage.

And no holy flesh ever went putrid: Holy things with a lower level of sanctity [Kodashim Kalim] that are eaten for two days and one night that were held for such a long time never went putrid.

And a High Priest did not have an accidental emission on Yom Kippur. so that would he not require the assistant. And even though they would know that he would not have an accidental emission, they [still] appointed an assistant; as we do not rely on miracles, because of - "Do not test" – as is found in the Yerushalmi Yoma.

And a fly was not seen in the room of slaughtering: due to its sanctity.

And there was not found a disqualification in the omer [a special barley offering, offered the day after Pesach, which permits grain harvested in the new harvest to be eaten]: No disqualification, of being outside the wall or held overnight, was ever found with the omer; which was at the time of barley, in order that all of Israel be permitted to eat new grain.

Or in the two breads: They come to permit bringing up the new offering form the new grain. And no disqualification, of being outside the courtyard or held overnight, was ever found with them.

Or in the showbreads: As it was arranged on Shabbat day, and it was warm at the time of its removal from the table as on the day that they placed it there - as it is stated - "to place warm bread on the day of its being taken." And no disqualification, of being outside the wall or being held over was ever found in it. As they needed to eat it during the week after the Shabbat that they took it away; but if it remained through another week it would become disqualified. And no mishap like this ever happened to them.

And rain did not extinguish the fire of the wood pile: As the fire burnt upon the outer altar which stood unprotected in the Tabernacle courtyard.

And the wind did not overpower the pillar of smoke: As it would billow straight up.

They would stand up crowded and bow down with enough space: They would stand in the courtyard all in rows, this one crowded next to the other; but they would bow down with space, such that not one of them would push his fellow.

And that is a wonder.

And a snake or scorpion never hurt a person in Jerusalem. Never.

And a person did not say to his fellow, "The place is too cramped that I should lodge in Jerusalem": When they went up to Jerusalem, he would not say, "The place is too crowded for me; make room for me to settle." And this is what David, peace be upon him, stated, - "Jerusalem that is built up, a city constructed together for it" - he wanted to say that when they built it, they measured it so that all of Israel could be contained in it. And the explanation of "for it" is for its sake; as it was for the sake of the congregation of Israel that would gather together that it was constructed.

6. Ten things were created on the eve of the Sabbath at twilight, and these are they: **1.** the mouth of the earth, **2.** the mouth of the well, **3.** the mouth of the donkey, **4.** the rainbow, **5.** the manna, **6.** the staff of Moses, **7.** the shamir, **8.** the letters, **9.** the writing, **10.** and the tablets. And some say: also, the demons, the grave of Moses, and the ram of Abraham, our father. And some say: and also, tongs, made with tongs.

Rabbeinu Yonah

Ten things were created on the eve of the first Shabbat at twilight. And these are they: The mouth of the earth for the swallowing of Korach and his assembly.

And the mouth of the well: The boulder that Moshe struck.

And the mouth of the donkey of Bilaam: - "And the Lord opened the mouth of the donkey".

And the rainbow: "My rainbow have I given in the cloud".

And the manna: of the wilderness.

And the staff of Moshe: with which he did the signs.

And the shamir: It was a type of long worm. And King Shlomo built the Temple with it, as he would place it on the stone and it would split. "And no hammer or ax or any iron tool was heard in the House while it was being built".

And the letters: The Torah that was written in front of God, may He be blessed, from the six days of Creation with black fire on top of white fire.

And the writing: The form of the letters carved on the

tablets.

And the tablets: themselves.

And some say, also the destructive spirits, and the burial place of Moshe: "And no man knew his burial place".

And the ram of Abraham, our father caught in the thicket by its horns; and Avraham went and took the ram and offered it up as a burnt offering in place of his son".

And some say, also the tongs, made with tongs: These are pincers with which a blacksmith holds metal when it is hot until he makes it into a vessel. And we learned - "Rabbi Yehuda says, 'Tongs can be fashioned only with other tongs, but who fashioned the first tongs? Rather, it was created by the hands of Heaven. They said to him, It is possible for one to make it in a mold and align it." And why was it necessary to count these ten things? To make known that all the Holy One, blessed be He, created, He created on condition that it change its nature when it is told to do so at a time when it is needed. As there is nothing from the depths, novel in the world that did not come up in the thought of God in the story of Creation. When the luminaries were suspended on the fourth day, He decreed upon them that they would stand for Yehoshua and Hizkiyahu; the sea, that it should split for the Children of Israel; and so on with all of them. However, these ten went up into His thought "on the eve of the first Shabbat at twilight," though they are included in the things that have change embedded in them.

7. There are seven things characteristic in a clod, and seven in a wise man: A wise man does not speak before one who is greater than he in wisdom, And does not break into his fellow's speech; And is not hasty to answer; He asks what is relevant, and he answers to the point; And he speaks of the first [point] first, and of the last [point] last; And concerning that which he has not heard, he says: I have not heard; And he acknowledges the truth. And the reverse of these [are characteristic] in a clod.

Rabbeinu Yonah

Seven things are found in a golem [an unformed person]: Anything the form of which has not been completed is called a golem, as it is stated - "Your eyes saw my unformed limbs [**golmi**]; they were all recorded in Your book" - before the formation of the limbs. So too, one who knows that which is taught to him, but does not know how to build an argument on his own is called a golem - as his wisdom is not recognizable. And his mind will never reach to fathom these seven things, some of which are from the topic of wisdom and some of which are from the good traits. And so, did Rambam, may his memory be blessed, explain.

And seven in a wise man. who knows how to build an? argument.

A wise man does not speak in front of someone who is greater than him in wisdom: As he listens, is quiet and learns; and in this way, he builds wisdom - which is not the case with the golem. As he does not desire understanding - but rather to reveal what is on his mind, as we wrote above.

And he does not interrupt the words of his fellow: but he allows him to speak until he finishes all of his words; and afterwards he gives him an answer. And that is a good trait.

But the golem does not do this, but answers something before he hears it.

And is not impulsive in answering: When they ask him, he is not quick to give an answer until he hears all of their claims and all that the questioners want to say and to elaborate on the question. Rather, he will study the words intently. And his mouth will not be impulsive and his heart will not be quick to put something out until it be clear as the sun in front of him. And this is from the way of wisdom, as this answer will be correct this way.

And he asks to the point and answers as is proper: Rabbi Meir Halevi, may his memory be blessed, explained, "he asks to the point": If he asks to get a reason for anything, he should only ask for a reason that is possible to give for that thing, according to the nature of that thing. And so too, if they ask him, he "answer as is proper".

And he speaks to the first point first and the last point last: And its explanation is not that he should answer about the first thing first, and about the last question last. Rather that if the first question is clarified by the last thing, he should elucidate that first, and then elucidate the first; so as to understand and clarify his answer and so that the thing will be assimilable for his listener. And that is why it is called first, even if it is last, because it precedes it logically and the first thing is clarified by it. And if the matter is the opposite, it is called last. And about this is it said, "to the first point first and the last point last." And this is from great wisdom and understanding of things. And the golem does not know from all of these things.

And about that which he has not heard anything, says, "I have not heard anything": About that which he has not heard from the mouth of his teacher, he should say, "I have not heard it from my teachers." And if he has a hypothesis about the thing, he should say, "But it appears to me like this." And this thing is from the good traits that the golem will not grasp.

And he concedes to the truth: Even if he is sufficiently wise to know how to respond with many claims and intelligent words and he can refute the claims of his fellow - since the latter is not as wise as he, he should not do so; if it appears to him that the truth is with the other. Rather he should concede to his words and not be concerned with victory, And it is honorable for him, since this is a beautiful and accepted trait. And the golem will not think about this, and it is a disgrace for him when he is defeated.

And their opposites are the case with a golem: As he will err in all of these, as he does not have the understanding of the wise man, as he is not whole in this disposition and in his wisdom.

8. Seven kinds of punishment come to the world for seven categories of transgression: When some of them give tithes, and others do not give tithes, a famine from drought comes some go hungry, and others are satisfied. When they have all decided not to give tithes, a famine from tumult and drought comes; When they have, in addition, decided not to set apart the dough-offering, an all-consuming famine comes. Pestilence comes to the world for sins punishable by death according to the Torah, but which have not been referred to the court, and for neglect of the law regarding the fruits of the sabbatical year. The sword comes to the world for the delay of judgment, and for the perversion of judgment, and because of those who teach the Torah not in accordance with the accepted law.

Rabbeinu Yonah

Seven kinds of punishment come to the world for seven categories of sin: When some of the people give tithes, and others do not give tithes, a famine from drought comes: A famine that comes because of the withholding of rains in their time.

And some go hungry, and others have plenty: This is poetic justice - "some of them give tithes, and others do not give tithes".

When they all decide not to give tithes: Since they all do not tithe:

A famine from tumult and drought comes: This is a famine that comes because of war and disasters that come to people and so they are not able to work their land. And the Lord will send tumult and they will all go hungry - poetic justice, as they all do not tithe.

And when they decide, in addition, not to set apart the dough offering: Since they all do not set apart the dough offering:

A famine of annihilation comes: A year that no rain falls at all - and the skies above your head shall be copper. Because of the proliferation of sins, there is a great punishment.

Pestilence comes to the world for the death penalties set forth in the Torah that are not given over to the court to carry out: For example, excision and death penalties at the hand of the Heavens.

And for violation of the laws governing the produce of the Sabbatical year: That he does not dispose of them from his house and does business with them and that is forbidden. And for this, pestilence comes from the angle that, the leaders of, Israel agreed to turn their eyes away from the community. In this which they are doing evil, pestilence comes to all of the haters of Israel - and from them, it extends to the whole world. However, if the heads do not have the power to protest against the lesser people, "pestilence comes to the world" is understood to be talking about an individual person - who is called a small world. And he is evil and will die in his sin. And all of Israel is then exempt.

The sword comes to the world: Since it is written - "I will bring a sword against you to wreak vengeance for the covenant." And covenant only means Torah, since it is written after it - "because and because they rejected My judgments.

And because of those who interpret the Torah counter to the accepted law: declaring the forbidden, permissible, and the permissible, forbidden.

9. Wild beasts come to the world for swearing in vain, and for the profanation of the Name. Exile comes to the world for idolatry, for sexual sins and for bloodshed, and for transgressing the commandment of the year of the release of the land. At four times pestilence increases: in the fourth year, in the seventh year and at the conclusion of the seventh year, and at the conclusion of the Feast of Tabernacles in every year. In the fourth year, on account of the tithe of the poor which is due in the third year. In the seventh year, on account of the tithe of the poor which is due in the sixth year; At the conclusion of the seventh year, on account of the produce of the seventh year; And at the conclusion of the Feast of Tabernacles in every year, for robbing the gifts to the poor.

Rabbeinu Yonah

Destructive animals come to the world because of false oaths: They sinned with the mouth - the teeth of beasts will I send upon them. As the difference between us and the beasts is in oral expression. And this is why we rule over them. And therefore, one who does not concern himself in this way for the glory of his Creator is fitting that he should be trampled by the beasts. And this is a cause for desecration of God's name, may He be blessed. As You adorned him with glory and majesty; You have made him master, and it is reversed - that the beasts will rule over the people that desecrate the glory of the Glorious one.

Exile comes to the world, etc.: And we learn all of them in the chapter entitled Bemeh Madlikin: As it is written about sexual prohibitions - "And the land became defiled; and I called it to account for its iniquity, and the land spewed out its inhabitants." And about idolatry, it is written - "and My soul will spurn [**gala**] you" - like a man who drives out his fellow from in front of him. As any ejection of something is called geeul. And about the sabbatical year, it is written - "Then shall the land make up for its sabbatical years throughout the time that it is desolate... it shall rest." And spilling of blood is even when accidental, and the proof of the thing is from the cities of refuge.

At four periods of time, etc.: As it is written - "Do not rob the poor, as he is poor." And is there something that can be robbed from the poor? Rather these are the gifts to the poor, since any one that withholds them and does not give them to the poor is as if he takes the soul life of the poor person. And he also robs the soul of the robber for himself, as it is written - "For the Lord will take up their cause and despoil those who despoil them their soul" - "their soul" being plural is meaning to say the soul of the robber and of the poor person. And therefore, pestilence increases and is common at these four periods of time - from the time that they hold on to the gifts.

In the fourth year it is because of the tithe to the poor in the third year: and they did not give it. As it is written - "At the end of three years, you shall bring out all the tithe, etc." And such is the order of the tithes.

And after the holiday Sukkot in every single year, it is because of the theft of gifts to the poor: As at the time of the holiday of Sukkot, it is the time of the harvest. And when they steal the gifts of the poor - as they do not leave over the dropped stalks, the forgotten stalks and the corners of the field - the Omnipresent punishes them immediately after their harvest. And therefore, it said, "At four periods of time, etc".

10. There are four types of character in human beings: One that says: "mine is mine, and yours is yours": this is a commonplace type; and some say this is a sodom-type of character. One that says: "mine is yours and yours is mine": is an unlearned person am haaretz; One that says: "mine is yours and yours is yours" is a pious person. One that says: "mine is mine, and yours is mine" is a wicked person.

Rabbeinu Yonah

There are four temperaments, etc.: the one who says "what is mine is mine, and what is yours is yours" He is not generous, but he is good in that he 'hates presents. And it is difficult. As how can they say that this is an average temperament? And is not someone who prevents himself from giving charity completely wicked? And granted that it is true that according to the one that says that it is the temperament of Sodom, it comes out well, as it is stated - "Behold this was the sin of your sister, Sodom, etc.; she did not support the poor and the needy." Rather, it is dealing with one who gives charity from fear of God, however his nature is to be stingy. And hence since he supports the poor and the needy,' what does his nature matter to us - the actual temperament in practice, is average. "And some say that it is the trait of Sodom" and that its source is very bad, since his nature is to be stingy. But regarding if he does not support the poor and the needy at all, everyone agrees about this that he is completely wicked and that it is the temperament of Sodom.

What is mine is yours, and what is yours is mine - that's an am ha'arets literally, a man of the land: Because this one wants the improvement of the world, he is called a man of the land. As he wants to give and to take, since love increases among them through this. And even if this is a good trait for the improvement of the world, this is not from wisdom. As one who hates presents shall live. And the good temperament is to give but not to take.

11. There are four kinds of temperments: Easy to become angry, and easy to be appeased: his gain disappears in his loss; Hard to become angry, and hard to be appeased: his loss disappears in his gain; Hard to become angry and easy to be appeased: a pious person; Easy to become angry and hard to be appeased: a wicked person.

Rabbeinu Yonah

A person who is easy to anger and easy to appease - his gain is canceled by his loss: As the loss is greater than the gain. As what is the use of his being appeased quickly, as long as his anger lay in his lap, and he will often come to sin. And who will be able to fix what he has made crooked during the time of his anger, even if he is quickly appeased.

A person who is hard to anger but also hard to appease - his loss is canceled by his gain: The gain is greater than the loss, since he only gets angry sporadically, for a great necessity. And even if he is not quickly appeased from that anger - behold, he is patient most of the time.

A person who is hard to anger, but easy to appease - that's a pious person: And it is not necessary that he never get angry, as sometimes a person needs to get angry out of zeal for God like Pinchas. Hence it said, "hard to anger," since he still needs to get angry - however it should be with difficulty at the times when he is not allowed to be without anger. And about this the wise men of ethics have said, "Do not be sweet, lest they swallow you up." And it is also a good thing to be appeased immediately - even when his anger is still upon him. And not after his anger has left him, but precisely at the time of his anger is he easy to appease - as this is from the trait of piety and good-heartedness.

12. There are four types of disciples: Quick to comprehend, and quick to forget: his gain disappears in his loss; Slow to comprehend, and slow to forget: his loss disappears in his gain; Quick to comprehend, and slow to forget: he is a wise man; Slow to comprehend, and quick to forget, this is an evil portion.

Rabbeinu Yonah

Quick to understand and quick to forget: His loss is greater. Since he forgets immediately, what is the use of that which he comprehends and knows quickly - behold, he forgets everything. But slow to understand and slow to forget: His gain is greater. As even if it comes to him with great toil, he does not forget after he knows it. And both of them should not desist from Torah study, as they have a good reward from their labor. And we learn from this mishnah to give preference to one who remembers over one who forgets - if they do not have enough to support both of them, they should support the one who remembers. This mishnah does not mention pious or wicked as it is not relevant here, since the mind of a person is from God. It is as the wise men of ethics said, "The mind is a gift, but character is acquired".

13. There are four types of charity givers. He who wishes to give, but that others should not give: his eye is evil to that which belongs to others; He who wishes that others should give, but that he himself should not give: his eye is evil towards that which is his own; He who desires that he himself should give, and that others should give: he is a pious man; He who desires that he himself should not give and that others too should not give: he is a wicked man.

Rabbeinu Yonah

There are four temperaments, etc.: One who wishes to give, but [that] others not give: He wants the good and the praise for himself and his want is not for the benefit of the creatures.

[One who wishes that] others give, and he [himself] not give: as he is stingy.

One who wishes to give and that others give: And this is what King Shlomo, peace be upon him, stated - "A generous soul" which is one that gives charity with a good eye "will prosper," but "one who benefits others" is greater, as he is one who benefits others and teaches them that they should give charity - as he wants to "give and that others give" - and this is the meaning of the end of the verse, "shall also be sated." And so too did Yishayahu state - "But the generous advises generosity and he stands upon generosity"; meaning to say, he advises himself to give, but he also stands on generosity - on the generosity of others who he tells to do like himself.

14. There are four types among those who frequent the study-house [bet midrash]: He who attends but does not practice: he receives a reward for attendance. He who practices but does not attend: he receives a reward for practice. He who attends and practices: he is a pious man; He who neither attends nor practices: he is a wicked man.

Rabbeinu Yonah

There are four temperaments, etc. One who goes but does not do: The intention is not that he does not do anything from that which he heard in the House of Study - as one who prevented himself from doing the commandments is completely wicked, even if he does not do sins. Rather, the intention is that he does not search for them in order to do them, but he rather does them by happenstance when they come to his hand.

One who does but does not go: to the House of Study to know the detail of the commandments and to be stringent about them - but he rather does them according to his limited knowledge - receives reward for this doing.

15. There are four types among those who sit before the sages: a sponge, a funnel, a strainer and a sieve. A sponge, soaks up everything; A funnel, takes in at one end and lets out at the other; A strainer, which lets out the wine and retains the lees; A sieve, which lets out the coarse meal and retains the choice flour.

Rabbeinu Yonah

There are four temperaments, etc. the sponge: This is a metaphor for a student who does not distinguish between a correct argument and one that is not, similar to a sponge that collects and absorbs water - whether it is dirty or whether it is clear.

The funnel: As it accepts all of the things, but loses them immediately.

The strainer: This is like a student that retains in his mind the argument that is incorrect and loses the correct one. And about this King Shlomo, peace be upon him, stated - "A man is praised according to his intelligence, but a twisted heart is disgraced" - that it is not fitting to disgrace one who knows less, but it is fitting to disgrace one whose heart is twisted. As this one's heart is twisted, in that he retains the thing that is incorrect - such that he is compared to a strainer, as it says.

The sieve, because it lets out the inferior flour: which is the incorrect argument; and does not retain it.

And retains the fine flour: meaning the correct argument, it retains it and does not lose it.

16. All love that depends on a something, when the thing ceases, the love ceases; and all love that does not depend on anything, will never cease. What is an example of love that depended on a something? Such was the love of Amnon for Tamar. And what is an example of love that did not depend on anything? Such was the love of David and Jonathan.

Rabbeinu Yonah

Any love etc. What's a love that is not dependent on something, etc. This is the love that has no interruption, even though a person estimates that some damage and disgrace will come to him from it, like the example of David and Jonathan. As even though Jonathan was fit to rise in the place of his father and David was going to remove him from the monarchy, nonetheless Jonathan loved him with a firm attachment. And that is what King David, peace be upon him said in his eulogy of Jonathan - "your love was wonderful to me than, which can also be read as, from the love of women." This is meaning to say, from where did I know that your love for me was wonderful? From the love of women. When he was the second to Shaul, the women had said - "Shaul has slain his thousands; David, his tens of thousands", and Shaul became jealous, as is known. However, it wasn't enough that Jonathan did not become jealous, but just the opposite - he saved him from the hand of his father. And this was from the angle that he loved him and it was not love of the body. And that is what is written - "and the soul of Jonathan was attached to the soul of David." However, the love of Amnon and Tamar is already clear and there is no need to elaborate.

17. Every dispute that is for the sake of Heaven, will in the end endure; But one that is not for the sake of Heaven, will not endure. Which is the controversy that is for the sake of Heaven? Such was the controversy of Hillel and Shammai. And which is the controversy that is not for the sake of Heaven? Such was the controversy of Korah and all his congregation.

<u>Rabbeinu Yonah</u>

Every argument, etc. This is to say about that which it said, "Every argument that is for the sake of heaven's name, it is destined to endure" - the intention is that they will endure in their argument forever. And so, today they will argue about one thing and tomorrow about another; and argument will endure and continue between them all the days of their lives. And not only this, but also length of days and years of life will be added to them.

But if it is not for the sake of heaven's name it is not destined to endure: Rather they will cease in their first argument. They will end and die there - as in the argument of Korach.

18. Whoever causes the multitudes to be righteous, sin will not occur on his account; And whoever causes the multitudes to sin, they do not give him the ability to repent. Moses was righteous and caused the multitudes to be righteous, therefore, the righteousness of the multitudes is hung on him, as it is said - "He executed the Lord's righteousness and His decisions with Israel". Jeroboam, sinned and caused the multitudes to sin, therefore, the sin of the multitudes is hung on him, as it is said, "For the sins of Jeroboam which he sinned, and which he caused Israel to sin thereby".

Rabbeinu Yonah

Anyone who brings merit to the many, sin does not result from him: So that his students not be in the Garden of Eden while he is in Gehinnom, as it is written - "For You will not abandon my soul to the grave, or let Your pious one sees the pit." And how is it possible that one who is pious should see the pit? Rather, since He is pious, He does not let him commit a sin - so that he should not see the pit on its account.

He fulfilled the righteousness of God and His statutes with Israel: This is to say that he completed and fulfilled the entire Torah - he and all of Israel with him.

19. Whoever possesses these three things, he is of the disciples of Abraham, our father; and whoever possesses three other things, he is of the disciples of Balaam, the wicked. A good eye, a humble spirit and a moderate appetite he is of the disciples of Abraham, our father. An evil eye, a haughty spirit and a limitless appetite he is of the disciples of Balaam, the wicked. What is the difference between the disciples of Abraham, our father, and the disciples of Balaam, the wicked? The disciples of Abraham, our father, enjoy this world, and inherit the world to come, as it is said: "I will endow those who love me with substance, I will fill their treasuries". But the disciples of Balaam, the wicked, inherit gehinnom, and descend into the nethermost pit, as it is said - "For you, O God, will bring them down to the nethermost pit those murderous and treacherous men; they shall not live out half their days; but I trust in You".

<u>Rabbeinu Yonah</u>

Anyone who has these three things, etc. It would have been possible for the tanna, author of this Mishnah, to be brief and not to elaborate by way of the category and the particulars. And he could have said, "Anyone who has a good eye, a humble spirit and a small appetite is from the students of Abraham, our father. An evil eye, a haughty spirit and a broad appetite - is from the students of Bilaam the evildoer." And why did he teach the general category and then go back to explain the particulars? Rather, he is coming to teach us that in these three things that he mentioned first are included all of the virtues, even if they have many parts; and so too the three things that are their opposites include all vice. And that is because if he had been brief in the way that he said it, it would have been understood that one who would have the three things mentioned is from the students of Abraham, our father; however, there would be many thousands and tens of thousands of virtues besides this to the students of Abraham, our father. And so therefore he first said that one who has these three things which he will mention - that is the student of Abraham our father. And afterwards, he explained that the students of Abraham, our father, are a good eye, etc. - which is to say, all of their virtue for which they were called the students of Abraham, our father, was a good eye, etc. And therefore, he does not say, "The students of Abraham, our father, had a good eye, etc." - meaning that they had these three things, even if they had many things like them. But by his saying "the students of Abraham, our father, are a good eye, etc.," he hinted that these three things were the causes of their being from the students of Abraham, our father, etc. And also, the opposite of this is the case with the students of Bilaam the evildoer. As he did not say, "the students of Bilaam had an evil eye, etc." - to teach that the essence of the teaching that they learned from Bilaam the evildoer were these three things, without any other evils. It is only these three things upon which they were students of Bilaam, since all of the evils were included in them - even if they have many parts.

Pirkei Avot - Rabbeinu Yonah - Chapter 5

20. Judah ben Tema said: Be strong as a leopard, and swift as an eagle, and fleet as a gazelle, and brave as a lion, to do the will of your Father who is in heaven. He used to say: the arrogant is headed for Gehinnom and the blushing for the garden of Eden. May it be the will, O Lord our God, that your city be rebuilt speedily in our days and set our portion in the studying of your Torah.

Rabbeinu Yonah

Yehudah ben Teimah says, etc. Be brazen like the leopard to rebuke those that commit sins; and to be much involved in Torah. You will not grow weary and grow faint. And so, did Yishayahu state - "But they who hope in the Lord shall renew their strength." When they grow weary, those that hope in the Lord shall have their strength increased and will renew it to be a new strength for them, with which to do the work of the Lord still longer.

light like the eagle: "Grow new wings like the eagles".

Swift like the deer: He wants to say, "They shall run and not grow weary." Other people get worn out when they run, but they do not get worn for the matter of a commandment. And so too, towards the matter of a commandment, "they shall march and not grow faint." As with other people, when one walks more than what he generally walks during the day, he is faint and grows weary.

And mighty like the lion: to become stronger towards the commandments. This is to say that all of his thought and the actions of his limbs be for the act of God.

To do the Will of your Father Who is in Heaven: This is to say, so long as it is in order to do the Will of your Father Who is in Heaven.

Brazen-faced: King Shlomo, peace be upon him, stated - "Guilt intercedes for fools" - as the evil fool will speak about the ugly thing and the guilty thing in a person when he sees them. That is like those imbeciles that said, "How foul is that carcass!" But, "among the upright, good will" - they only speak about the praise and the good will. It is like the wise man said regarding the same carcass, "How white are its teeth"!

21. He used to say: At five years of age the study of Scripture; At ten the study of Mishnah; At thirteen subjects to the commandments; At fifteen the study of Talmud; At eighteen the bridal canopy; At twenty for pursuit of livelihood; At thirty the peak of strength; At forty wisdom; At fifty able to give counsel; At sixty old age; At seventy fullness of years; At eighty the age of "strength"; At ninety a bent body; At one hundred, as good as dead and gone completely out of the world.

Rabbeinu Yonah

He used to say, etc. Ninety is the age for a bending stature lashuach: This is related to the expression, pit [**shiach**] and cave, meaning to say that he is fit for burial. And some explain it is from the expression, **siach** speaking, as he should only be occupied by words of Torah - since his days are close to dying.

22. Ben Bag Bag said: Turn it over, and [again] turn it over, for all is therein. And look into it; And become gray and old therein; And do not move away from it, for you have no better portion than it.

Rabbeinu Yonah

Search in it, etc.: Review the words of Torah, as all the wisdom of the world is included in it.

23. Ben He He said: According to the labor is the reward.

Rabbeinu Yonah

Ben Bag Bag says, etc.: Since above it warns severely about Torah study and even until old age and hoary-headedness, and even if it causes great pain and it weakens his strength, he should not move from it; Ben Hey Hey comes to console a person and to speak to his heart, that he should not be concerned about his great pain, as According to the pain is the reward.

Pirkei Avot - Rabbeinu Yonah - Chapter 6

Rabbeinu Yonah did not interpret this chapter, nor did Maimonides. It seems to me that this chapter is not from the Tannaim, but from the Amoraim.

Chapter 6 פרק ו'

1. The sages taught in the language of the mishnah. Blessed be He who chose them and their teaching. Rabbi Meir said: Whoever occupies himself with the Torah for its own sake, merits many things; not only that but he is worth the whole world. He is called beloved friend; one that loves God; one that loves humankind; one that gladdens God; one that gladdens humankind. And the Torah clothes him in humility and reverence, and equips him to be righteous, pious, upright and trustworthy; it keeps him far from sin, and brings him near to merit. And people benefit from his counsel, sound knowledge, understanding and strength, as it is said, "Counsel is mine and sound wisdom; I am understanding, strength is mine" - And it bestows upon him royalty, dominion, and acuteness in judgment. To him are revealed the secrets of the Torah, and he is made as an ever-flowing spring, and like a stream that never ceases. And he becomes modest, long-suffering and forgiving of insult. And it magnifies him and exalts him over everything.

2. Rabbi Joshua ben Levi said: every day a bat kol **A heavenly voice** goes forth from Mount Horeb and makes proclamation and says: "Woe unto

humankind for their contempt towards the Torah", for whoever does not occupy himself with the study of Torah is called, nazuf, the rebuked. As it is said, "Like a gold ring in the snout of a pig is a beautiful woman bereft of sense" - And it says, "And the tablets were the work of God, and the writing was the writing of God, graven upon the tablets" - Read not haruth '**graven**' but heruth '**freedom**'. For there is no free man but one that occupies himself with the study of the Torah. And whoever regularly occupies himself with the study of the Torah he is surely exalted, as it is said, "And from Mattanah to Nahaliel; and Nahaliel to Bamoth".

3. One who learns from his fellow one chapter, or one halakhah, or one verse, or one word, or even one letter, is obligated to treat him with honor; for so we find with David, king of Israel, who learned from Ahitophel no more than two things, yet called him his master, his guide and his beloved friend, as it is said, "But it was you, a man mine equal, my guide and my beloved friend" - Is this not [an instance of the argument] "from the less to the greater" (kal vehomer)? If David, king of Israel who learned from Ahitophel no more than two things, nevertheless called him his master, his guide and his beloved friend; then in the case of one who learns from his fellow one chapter, or one halakhah, or one verse, or one word, or even one letter, all the more so he is under obligation to treat him with honor. And "honor'" means nothing but Torah, as it is said, "It is honor that sages inherit" - "And the perfect shall inherit good" - and "good" means nothing but

Torah, as it is said - "For I give you good instruction; do not forsake my Torah".

4. Such is the way of a life of Torah: you shall eat bread with salt, and rationed water shall you drink; you shall sleep on the ground, your life will be one of privation, and in Torah shall you labor. If you do this, "Happy shall you be and it shall be good for you" - "Happy shall you be" in this world, "and it shall be good for you" in the world to come.

5. Do not seek greatness for yourself, and do not covet honor. Practice more than you learns. Do not yearn for the table of kings, for your table is greater than their table, and your crown is greater than their crown, and faithful is your employer to pay you the reward of your labor.

6. Greater is learning Torah than the priesthood and than royalty, for royalty is acquired by thirty stages, and the priesthood by twenty-four, but the Torah by forty-eight things. By study, Attentive listening, Proper speech, By an understanding heart, By an intelligent heart, By awe, By fear, By humility, By joy, By attending to the sages, By critical give and take with friends, By fine argumentation with disciples, By clear thinking, By study of Scripture, By study of mishnah, By a minimum of sleep, By a minimum of chatter, By a minimum of pleasure, By a minimum of frivolity, By a minimum of preoccupation with worldly matters, By long-suffering, By generosity, By faith in the sages, By acceptance of suffering. Learning of Torah is also acquired by one Who recognizes his place, Who rejoices in his portion, Who makes a fence about his words, Who takes no credit for himself, Who is loved, Who loves God, Who loves his fellow creatures, Who loves righteous ways, Who loves reproof, Who loves uprightness, Who keeps himself far from honors, Who does not let his heart become swelled on account of his learning, Who does not delight in giving legal decisions, Who shares in the bearing of a burden with his colleague, Who judges with the scales weighted in his favor, Who leads him on to truth, Who leads him on to peace, Who composes himself at his study, Who asks and answers, Who listens to others, and himself adds to his knowledge, Who learns in order to teach, Who learns in order to practice, Who makes his teacher wiser, Who is exact in what he has learned, And who says a thing in the name of him who said it. Thus, you have learned: everyone who says a thing in the name of him who said it, brings deliverance into the world, as it is said: "And Esther told the king in Mordecai's name".

7. Great is Torah for it gives life to those that practice it, in this world, and in the world to come, As it is said - "For they are life unto those that find them, and health to all their flesh", And it says: "It will be a cure for your navel and marrow for your bones" And it says: "She is a tree of life to those that grasp her, and whoever holds onto her is happy", And it says: "For they are a graceful wreath upon your head, a necklace about your throat", And it says: "She will adorn your head with a graceful wreath; crown you with a glorious diadem" And it says: "In her right hand is length of days, in her left riches and honor" And it says: "For they will bestow on you length of days, years of life and peace".

8. Rabbi Shimon ben Menasya said in the name of Rabbi Shimon ben Yohai: Beauty, strength, riches, honor, wisdom, old age, gray hair, and children are becoming to the righteous, and becoming to the world, As it is said: "Gray hair is a crown of glory beauty; it is attained by way of righteousness" it says: "The ornament of the wise is their wealth" And it says: "The glory of youths is their strength; and the beauty of old men is their gray hair", And it says: "Grandchildren are the glory of their elders, and the glory of children is their parents", And it says: "Then the moon shall be ashamed, and the sun shall be abashed. For the Lord of Hosts will reign on Mount Zion and in Jerusalem, and God's Honor will be revealed to his elders". Rabbi Shimon ben Menasya said: these seven qualities, which the sages have listed as becoming to the righteous, were all of them fulfilled in Rabbi and his sons.

9. Rabbi Yose ben Kisma said: Once I was walking by the way when a man met me, and greeted me and I greeted him. He said to me, "Rabbi, where are you from?" I said to him, "I am from a great city of sages and scribes". He said to me, "Rabbi, would you consider living with us in our place? I would give you a thousand thousand denarii of gold, and precious stones and pearls." I said to him: "My son, even if you were to give me all the silver and gold, precious stones and pearls that are in the world, I would not dwell anywhere except in a place of Torah; for when a man passes away there accompany him neither gold nor silver, nor precious stones nor pearls, but Torah and good deeds alone, as it is said, "When you walk it will lead you. When you lie down it will watch over you; and when you are awake it will talk with you". "When you walk it will lead you" in this world. "When you lie down it will watch over you" in the grave; "And when you are awake it will talk with you" in the world to come. And thus, it is written in the book of Psalms by David, king of Israel, "I prefer the teaching You proclaimed to thousands of pieces of gold and silver", And it says: "Mine is the silver, and mine the gold, says the Lord of Hosts".

10. Five possessions did the Holy Blessed One, set aside as his own in this world, and these are they:The Torah, one possession; Heaven and earth, another possession; Abraham, another possession; Israel, another possession; The Temple, another possession. The Torah is one possession. From where do we know this? Since it is written, "The Lord possessed [usually translated as **created**] me at the beginning of his course, at the first of His works of old" Heaven and earth, another possession. From where do we know this? Since it is said: "Thus said the Lord: The heaven is My throne and the earth is My footstool; Where could you build a house for Me, What place could serve as My abode? And it says: "How many are the things You have made, O Lord; You have made them all with wisdom; the earth is full of Your possessions" Abraham is another possession. From where do we know this? Since it is written: "He blessed him, saying, "Blessed by Abram of God Most High, Possessor of heaven and earth" Israel is another possession. From where do we know this? Since it is written: "Till Your people cross over, O Lord, Till Your people whom You have possessed". And it says: "As to the holy and mighty ones that are in the land, my whole desire possession is in them" The Temple is another possession. From where do we know this? Since it is said: "The sanctuary, O lord, which your hands have established", And it says: "And He brought them to His holy realm, to the mountain, which His right hand had possessed".

11. Whatever the Holy Blessed One created in His world, he created only for His glory, as it is said: "All who are linked to My name, whom I have created, formed and made for My glory", And it says: "The Lord shall reign for ever and ever".

Said Rabbi Hananiah ben Akashya: It pleased the Holy Blessed One to grant merit to Israel, that is why He gave them Torah and commandments in abundance, as it is said, "The Lord was pleased for His righteousness, to make Torah great and glorious".

www.ingramcontent.com/pod-product-compliance
Lightning Source LLC
Chambersburg PA
CBHW070134080526
44586CB00015B/1687